The Finn Chronicles:
Year Three

A dog's reports from the front lines of hooman rescue

by Finnegan Count Smooshie Tushie
as transcribed by Gwen Romack

Published by Off Leash Press

For information contact Gwen Romack:
thesquishyone@thefinnchronicles.com

ISBN: 978-1-7352473-4-2

I dedicate this book to my Squishy One and my Hairy One for making a miserable year of quarantine a little less miserable. Their dedication to fun games, careful playdates and constant attention made our pandemic year a little more tolerable.
#IMissTheConstantAdoration

I also appreciate all the people working on the front lines of this mess and the people taking it seriously to protect the vulnerable hoomans like my Squishy One.
#WeGottaStickTogetherHoomans

Also, bacon.

Contents

Introduction

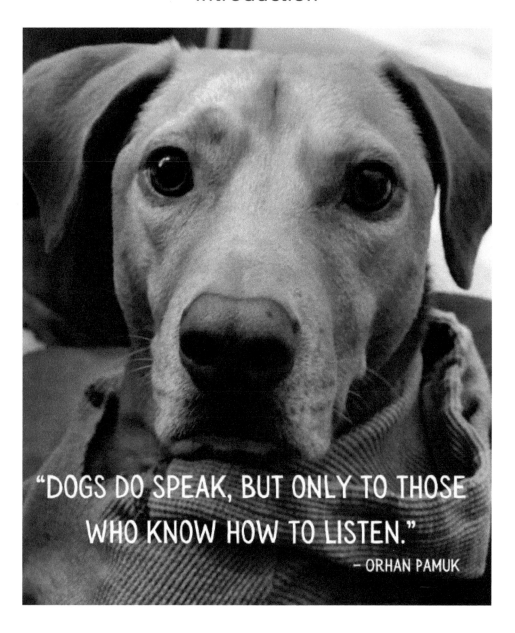

"DOGS DO SPEAK, BUT ONLY TO THOSE WHO KNOW HOW TO LISTEN."

– ORHAN PAMUK

My name is Finnegan Count Smooshie Tushie, but I go by Finn for short. I'm a mix of the regal and intense Hungarian Vizsla, the vocal and intense Beagle, and the sensitive and stubborn Pittie. Basically, a perfect combination of intensity, volume and sensitivity.

As a top graduate of the K9 Rescue Academy, I was given some really challenging hoomans for my rescue assignment. I write reports back to rescue headquarters that they use to halp train the younger cadets and update our files about the hoomans and their strange rituals. It's been a challenge training these hoomans, but I've come to love them. I've got a hairy hooman I call Daddy and a squishy hooman I call Mommy.

This book includes my third year of reports and adventures. You should go back and read the first two years if you haven't already. We lay the groundwork for critical philosophical and mathematical theorems in those books that you need to understand before proceeding to this one. No, not really. But it does halp you get to know me and my hoomans.

I've got The Squishy One doing the social media for me and a FinnTube channel where you can find videos that go along with some of my finnanigans in this book! There's also loads of bonus content for endless fun and cuteness.

My website:
https://www.thefinnchronicles.com

FinnTube:
https://www.youtube.com/c/FinnTheDog
(Check out the *Year Three Playlist* for videos that you'll recognize from the stories. These are linked throughout in the ebook version, but you can also find them all at the FinnTube link above.)

Week One Hundred Six

March 21, 2020 ·

HI EVERYONE. FINN HERE with my week 106 report. This week was filled with strange rituals and a splash of horrific, unnecessary and wholly disrespectful trauma. #ABaff

The freaks spent a lot of time this week carrying on about four leaf clovers, green food, and leprechauns. I was forced to wear a ridiculous hat and smile for the camera. #SpoilerAlertIDidntSmile #ImHungarianNotIrishYouFools

On the plus side, I tried a new foodstuff the Squishy One called "cabbage," and it was tasty. At first, I thought it was just for shredding, like carrots. But then I noticed it tasted pretty good and ate my shredded scraps. The hoomans were worried I might have thunderbutt from it later that evening, but I didn't. #CantSayTheSameForThem

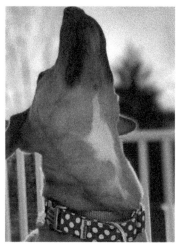

I got serious about my oversight of the Hairy One's work one night. I couldn't see the screen well enough from where I was sitting, so I skooched up just a little. He got all snippy and said I was micromanaging him. I said zip it and do the bang bang on keyboard with less lip. #IWouldntHaveToMicromanageIfYouDidBetter #QualityControl #IllDoTheThinkingAroundHere

Then we had a fairly heated 1x1 about his performance. I followed the HR training for giving constructive feedback, but he didn't follow the training on how to receive it. I used lots of personal accountability "I" statements such as, "I think you smell and should give me more attention." He's a big baby, and we ended up in a fight that escalated

to involve HR, again. #HesSuchAWhiner
#WaitTilHeHearsIveBeenPromotedAgain

In what was obvious passive aggressive retaliation, he lured me into the wet room with treats then trapped me in that awful, no good, burns-my-soul shower and got me wet. Then he rubbed me with towels, a clear signal for play, but got mad when I bit him. I mean the towel… I bit the towel. #YouCantProveAnything #IPreferActiveAggressiveOverPassive

I escalated to the HR VP (Mommy), and she tried to smooth things over with a team meeting on the deck. Nothing unites the Hairy One and me faster than our mutual dislike of her hippy-dippy role play, "me statements" and the share-your-feelings stick. We roll our eyes so hard when she isn't looking, sometimes I think they may pop out. She always wants us to find things we can agree on. #WeAgreeShesAFreak

That's all the news and #Finnanigans from this week. Over and out.

Week One Hundred Seven

March 28, 2020 ·

HI EVERYONE. FINN HERE with my week 107 report. The hoomans have been staying home nearly all the time now for three weeks. #TheyCantGetEnoughOfMe The Hairy One leaves once a week to hunt and gather hooman food stuffs, but that's it. Finally, my training efforts are paying off. #MoreFocusOnMeThanks

I haven't been to camp in three weeks though, and I'm starting to lose it. Honestly, I think they are, too. I watched the Squishy One cut holes in a box for hours. She was cussing some and mumbling to herself while she made the holes. Then the Hairy One got down on the floor with the box and

kept showing me a hot dog through the holes. It would seem Daddy's job was to move the hot dog around and my job was to catch it. They laughed and laughed. #Perplexing #WhyYouFreaks #IJustPlayAlong

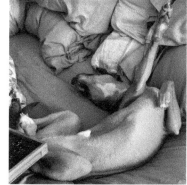

I can only imagine what the voices in her head were telling her that got this whole thing started. The next day it happened again, but this time with a carrot. My job is to shred carrots all over the carpet, not chase carrots. But I can't do my job if I can't capture the carrot. Spoiler alert: I did capture the carrot. #HeyWhatsBackHere

Walkies in the neighborhood have been nice. It's getting warm enough again to go for extra-long walkies. On one walk, out of nowhere, we encountered what I believe was a robin bird. It was terrifying!! I saved the hoomans from the dangerous robin with an impressive standup bark. #IExcelAtBarkingAndStandingUp

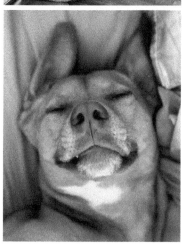

I finally convinced the Squishy One to start working on my book deal and to step up my social media status. I finally have my own Facebook and Instagram pages. I'm tired of her stealing my glory on her pages. She says I don't use hashtags right, and I'm gonna crash the internet. #WhatsSheKnow #ImGonnaBeFamous

She's working on editing my book and getting it ready to publish (two years late!). I'm also on her case about getting my blog website up. #ShesSoSlowButShesFree

That's all the news and #Finnanigans from this week. Over and out.

Special Report

March 29, 2020 ·

I find active play halps remind the hoomans who's dominant and burns their energy. #NoBites #MustBite

Week One Hundred Eight

April 4, 2020 ·

HI EVERYONE. FINN HERE with my week 108 report. What happens to things when they go inside the vroomswoosh and rumble machines? The hoomans put their clothes in there all the time, but I don't know why. All I know is they go in smelling perfectly stinky and glorious and come out smelling disgusting and clean. Normally I wouldn't care but I need to know how to halp Captain Ducky cope with his trauma after his time in there. #HesActingWeird #100YardStare

Mommy said she was just gonna duckysit a while to give me some *me* time. Then I caught her putting the ole Cap'n in the swoosher thing. I stood vigil until he emerged, fluffy, clean and underweight. He lost a lot of weight in there, from stress, I guess. #Bamboozled #SheCantBeTrusted #SomeMightCallHimAFeatherWeight

I saved their lives again this week and as usual, just got barked at. They are never grateful for my life saving efforts. See, I spotted these Canadian geese quacking and flying in the forward air space with obvious intent to invade the backyard air space. I barked a fierce warning then ran like a missile to the back door to keep them out of our air space. My Daddy was grilling back there!!! #ImminentDanger #ThreatLevel10 I stood up on my back legs to be more menacing, but I forgot the screen was there when I came back down. Apparently, shredding the

screen is frowned upon here.
#ThereWasCussing
#ThatScreenDidntSaveHimIDid

After the swearing and laughing died down, the Squishy One gave me a "thank you, I'm sorry" treat hidden in a small forest of felt things. She amused herself hiding my yum yums then watching me hunt for them. Why are they always hiding my treats in weird places? She called this one a Snufflemat and wouldn't let me shred the little trees.
#ThatWouldMakeItMoreFunThough

The hoomans are doing a lot of jigsaw puzzles and won't let me halp. They said I need thumbs. I showed them just how many pieces I could move without thumbs.
#AnytimeIMakeThemCussImWinning

I engaged the Hairy One in lots of active play this week to keep his spirits up and maintain dominance. He pretends he doesn't like it when I chew on his ear, and I chew more. He yells "no bites" and I bark "mmmust biiiiites." We wrestle until someone gets hurt and Mommy ends the fun. I think it's important to remind him who's alpha and sometimes I let him think it's him.
#WeBothLetMommyThinkItsHer
#Hilarious

Antler training was going pretty well until I got cocky. You'll see in the video that I'd gotten the hoomans trained to hold my antler for me, just how I like, whenever I wanted. But then I showed the video to some hoomans who told Mommy antlers can break my teefs. And now I don't have any more antlers. #RatFinks #SnitchesGetStitches

I woke the hoomans this morning just after sunrise to express my displeasure about the stolen antlers. I started mumbling around 5 but didn't go full melt down until after 6. #TheyThinkPretendingToBeAsleepWillStopMe #ItDoesnt

That's all the news and #Finnanigans from this week. Over and out.

Week One Hundred Nine

April 11, 2020 ·

HI EVERYONE. FINN HERE with my week 109 report. It's been another week of non-stop hoomaning. They just won't leave. I used to get a few hours a week to just relax. Watch a little Animal Planet, lick what needs lickin' and lounge around uninterrupted. Now it's constant walks, pretending I'm something called "ET," and strange conversations about someone realizing the word Saturday has the word "turd" in it. They're also making me listen to videos of some annoying dog screaming and howling all the time! #TheyreCrackingUp

They've been banging on their glowing screen things and talking to imaginary people a lot. The Squishy One has had a few of those "meetings", as she calls them, and I've halped myself to her lap, you know... to comfort her. She's hearing voices, after all. She said when her imaginary friends see me on the glowing screen thing it makes them laugh. #SureItDoesMama #WhateverYouSayYouFreak

I've begun interrupting glowing screen time with aggressive licking. If she won't put it away and focus on me, I gently nudge it until it falls off her lap, making room for me. That got me yelled at a few times. So, I've adjusted my technique to slow but aggressive licking of any exposed skin until she has to put it down to make me stop. #SheHatesMyLicks #IfAProblemComesAlongYouMustLickIt

I've been trying to halp rehab Cap'n Ducky from his traumatic experience getting clean. I snuck him into the yard

and smushed him into the mulch to get some nice color on him. He loved it. #TheHairyOneDidnt Then I brought him inside to Mommy and crawled into bed for snuggles. A few minutes later she was screaming and yelling about something called, "OMG ANTS!!" #ImStillInvestigatingTheSource

The Hairy One and I enjoyed a nice carry-cuddle the other morning, and the hoomans' creepy security cameras caught the whole thing. Now the Squishy One is jealous and whining about how he loves me more than her. #WellDuh

I've been training the Squishy One to pull up the covers for me to jump into bed and nestle between her legs. She's finally catching on and complying. I like to wake up at random hours overnight and decide it's time to go undercover. I go to her side of the bed and shove my cold snoozle onto her warm bum or arm - whatever is exposed. If that doesn't work, I start flailing the covers around for emphasis. Sometimes she pretends she is asleep and can't hear me. But we all know that's a lie. Eventually, she holds up the covers and I jump into bed. I like to curl up between her legs so she can't move at night. #ColdSnoozleWarmHeart

I've also been having some issues with the broom this week. The hoomans assure me it's safe and has lived here longer than me. But, I'm dubious. It keeps staring at me in a threatening way and making comments about my hair shedding so much lately. #ItsSpringICantHalpIt

That's all the news and #Finnanigans from this week. Over and out.

Week One Hundred Ten

April 18, 2020 ·

HI EVERYONE. FINN HERE with my week 110 report. The hoomans told me that the Easter Bunny couldn't come here for my annual Easter egg hunt and bring me a basket of goodies because of Coronavirus. Then I hop on Finnbook and Finnstagram and what do I see? The Easter Bunny all over the place!!! #Betrayal #Liars #ThisIsWhyIHaveTrustIssues

Then they dragged me into the horrible wet room for another baff for no reason! I didn't even roll in glorious poop this time. They claim it's to halp with my pollen allergies. But, see also: Easter Bunny! #PantsOnFire #WhatsPollen

The Squishy One felt bad that I was angry after the baff. So, she let me snuggle in her spot on the bed and watch an animal-scape movie. I mostly refused eye contact with her until the elephant roared! It ended when the birds flew across, and I ran through the house barking at every window to find them. #NotOnMyWatchSkyRats

It's otherwise been a pretty quiet week here at Chez Finn. The Squishy One didn't feel good, so we slept and snuggled a lot. I was her ever-vigilant nurse, monitoring her vitals while we snoozled by pressing my nose against her neck. And as per protocol, I laid across her torso with all my body weight to prevent movement. #ImHereToHalp

She also spent a lot of time this week playing with her yarn stuffs. See also:

ignoring me. She says she's making halpful things for the essential workers. But when she's playing with her yarn stuff, she is not petting me or using her paws to make me yum yums. This is unacceptable. I threw a pretty good fit to demonstrate my displeasure.
#ISingTheSongOfMyPeopleToShowIveBeenWronged

Also here is a video of another protest when I got short changed on my post-dinner walk. During this protest, the fireplace snuck up on me and scared me.
#WhenDidThatGetThere

That's all the news and #Finnanigans from this week. Over and out.

Special Report
April 18, 2020 ·

Sometimes I fall asleep sniffing my own butt. #BecauseICan

Week One Hundred Eleven

April 25, 2020 ·

#WhatInTheBaffTubIsGoingOnHere

HI EVERYONE. FINN HERE with my week 111 report. As we all know, the value of a toy goes up exponentially when a hooman wants it, threatens to get it, or touches it. #ScientificallyProven

This relates to scarcity, supply and demand, and other complicated factors. I encountered two strange anomalies this week that have interrupted the scarcity dynamic and created significant pack confusion: a second Captain Ducky and a second red rubber tire toy.

It all started when the Squishy One decided to finally let me explore Mr. Snuggles' old toy basket. He was their last rescue leader, and from the smell of things, he was awesome. His huge basket of toys stays hidden in a secret closet, and they never let me have them! They claim it's because I swallow what I kill and that could lead to emergency surgery. #LikelyStory

Anyway, the Squishy One just lost her marbles one day this week and put the basket in the middle of the room. She nodded and said ok, but at first, I was worried it was a trap. I made my way closer, and she didn't make a move or yell. Calculating the risk-to-reward ratio, I made my move!! I buried my face into the pile as far as it would go and took a long and very satisfying sniff. So many glorious smells, I was overcome with joy. Then I started removing toys one at a time until the whole basket was empty. It was so much fun!!! #Jackpot

The confusion started when I found an imposter Captain Ducky in the big basket. But this ducky was clean and had all its flappy things still intact. I inquired with the real Captain Ducky who said he didn't know who the imposter was. We've been thinking it over all week and concluded the only logical explanation is a twin brother separated at hatch. We decided it wasn't imposter ducky's fault and welcomed him into our pack at the rank of Corporal. #CorporalDucky

Then I found a second rubber tire toy! What is this madness? Perhaps an anomaly in the space-time continuum? A fold in space that created a duplicate red rubber tire existing in the same plane? This is the most plausible explanation.
#WeAreWatchingALotOfStarTrekLately

I had to get ugly a few nights in a row at dinner o'clock. At one point I even had to chew on the ottoman (aka my window throne) to get the hoomans' attention.
#WhyDoTheyTestMeSo

The Squishy One gave me two new foodstuffs this week. Update: Oranges are nummy; celery is not. #ILikeNewFoodStuffs

That's all the news and #Finnanigans from this week. Over and out.

Special Report

April 27, 2020 ·

Morning staff meeting is boring. I'm tuning out and day dreaming of squirrels.

Week One Hundred Twelve

May 2, 2020 ·

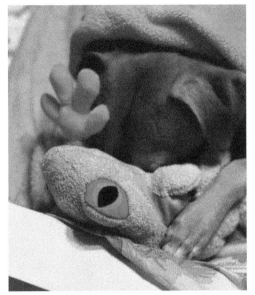

HI EVERYONE. FINN HERE with my week 112 report. I got to leave the house and go for a ride!!!!!!!! It was different than usual, but I got to go see my friends at Coastal Vet!! Daddy said because of the virus stuff he had to stay in the car. We had to wait forever for someone to come get me. (Mommy says this is one of her favorite videos, ever.) A nice tech came and got me, and I was so excited I hopped on my back legs all the way to the front door. Then another tech came out to put something in a basket, and I knocked the basket out of her hands trying to sniffestigate. Once inside I jumped on everyone I saw so they could give me proper lovin's and kisses. Dr. Richards called my Mommy and I heard her say I was perfectly perfect in every way. #Duh But my ears have been really extra itchy this spring, so they gave me a pinchy shot. She said I won't need my pills after each meal anymore. #ButIIIStillGetThePillPocketsRight

Then I heard Mommy say something to Dr. Richards about peanut butter and my face itching really bad. Then I heard Dr. Richards say no more peanut butter for Finn. I blacked out from shock and horror after that, but came to back in the car with Daddy. #ImSureSheDidntMeanIt #SheHathBetrayedMe

The next night, I was delighted to see the Squishy One with my cherished licky licky mat in her hands. Oh, the glorious sticky peanut butter bliss. I ran over, excited for my lick-fest to begin, only to find some frozen plain yogurt on there! #Betrayal #DevilWoman #WhatInTheBaffTubIsThis #HardPass #GimmeTheGoodStuff

Things with the Squishy One have been annoying all week. She is bored and practicing balancing things on my head. I do not enjoy this, but I let her have her fun. I have a hard boundary at foodstuffs, though. There will be no treats or other foodstuffs balanced on my head. #TrainingHerIsHard

She's also been playing with balls of yarn for weeks. She says she is crocheting ear savers for essential workers, but if hands are crocheting, they aren't petting me, preparing me food, or fetching me toys. She's not even a cat! #Unacceptable I found an excellent way to interrupt this is to lay across her belly and put my head on the yarn. She kept going one night even though the yarn moving against my face kept making me jump and squirm. We dug in on our respective positions, unwilling to budge. That was until the yarn touched my paw, and I jumped off her lap in terror. IT TOUCHED MY PAW. #ShesExhausting #IAlmostDied

She did get some good pictures of me with the Hairy One and also with Froggy Frog. #ImAdorable

That's all the news and #Finnanigans from this week. Over and out.

Week One Hundred Thirteen

May 9, 2020 ·

HI EVERYONE. FINN HERE with my week 113 report. It's been a decent week here at Chez Finn. The Squishy One finally got my FinnTube channel going, and I just know I'm on the brink of fame and fortune. I can't wait to be carried around on a satin pillow from guest spot to guest spot on Ellen, Jimmy Fallon and Kelly Clarkson. I bet Ellen will tell me I'm the cutest. #CuzIAm

We had a pretty intense morning staff meeting that got heated. I brought up the lack of treats in the break room, and the Hairy One claimed we had to start rationing. Captain Ducky and I escalated to HR (the Squishy One), and she said it was true – rationing is necessary until the next grocery run. I don't know what rationing is, but it sounds like not getting what I want. #ThisIsIntolerable #WhosForUnlimitedSnacksInTheBreakRoom #IMayNeedToFormAUnionSoon

I've had great success with the hoomans' training around evening hungry time. They are now pretty well settled on the routine. I cry, scream, chortle, and side-eye until they realize it's hungry o'clock. Then someone asks me "where do good dogs go?" and I run, hop, skip and pirouette into my special place. #WithPizzazz I then anxiously await meal preparation. If you look closely at the video, you can see why this is important. #SoMuchDrool The Squishy One says my drool is so slippery, she's slipped on the wood floors. #LikeBabyOilOnGlass #WhoTurnedOnTheFaucet

The Squishy One and I had some quality deck time before a big storm blew in. It was sunny and windy. I like the way the wind brings me smells to smell. Even though it's hot and sweaty, I insist on laying on top of the Squishy One to soothe her and remind her who's boss. #BecauseICare #SheLovesIt #FurBlanketOnASunnyDay

The low point of the week has been the reemergence of a stupid "game" these idiots think I want to play. When they did this last year, I was just a young puppy. I was so afraid of the bottles it took me a week to get up the nerve to swat or bite at them. Once I did, the treats came flowing out and I was victorious. But now I'm older and wiser. I will not play these silly games. I watched the Squishy One wash and dry the bottles, then carefully cut the holes – and I wondered what she was up to. Then I watched the hoomans set up the contraption and sighed my loudest, disapproving, why-do-you-do-this-to-me sigh. Then they started yelling at me to "get it." Nooo, YOU get it, Devil Woman!! They put the treats in there,

so why should I have to get them? #AndTheyHaveThumbs Anyway, you can see the whole evening of attempts on the long video on my FinnTube channel. She's tickled with herself to have learned how to add subtitles. #EyeRoll

What she didn't catch on video was my brilliant idea. In between takes and yelling at me to "get it," I walked over to the counter where the bag of treats was sitting, jumped up and nudged them with my nose. I tried to explain a major process improvement here would be to just put them directly from the bag into my treat hole. #TheyAreDumb

One of my toys got trapped under the bed and I screamed for halp. The video shows me clearly asking for halp until the Squishy finally asks if I need halp (Hello… yes you fool!), and I very cutely answer. And if you watch closely, you can see me put my arm on top of Daddy's as we head under there together to get it. #TeamworkMakesTheDreamWork

Mommy and I also enjoyed some TV time in bed one morning, and I got to pick the channel. I went for Animal Planet, of course. #LotsOfBirdsWaitingToBeChased

That's all the news and #Finnanigans from this week. Over and out.

Week One Hundred Fourteen

May 16, 2020 ·

HI EVERYONE. FINN HERE with my week 114 report. By far, the highlight of the week was counter-surfing to steal my new fren. As soon as I saw her come out of the box I knew she was going to be my buddy. I tried to wait patiently for the Squishy One to give her to me, but she took too long. So I got all my brave organized into one burst of speed and stole her! #YaGottaDoWhatYaGottaDo

I've named her Karen, and when she squeaks I cry. This gives me anxiety that makes me want to chew on her. That makes her squeak, then I cry more. It's a vicious cycle. #StopCryingKaren

My allergies are calming down a little thanks to Dr. Richards, and I'm loving more outside time. Mommy snapped some great pictures of Daddy and me playing, "Finn, Drop. Drop. Fiiiinnnnnn, Drooooooop!" with some grass in my treat hole. I love eating grass and sometimes barfing it up later on the Squishy One. #StopItSheLovesIt

He loves sticking his big meaty paws into my mouf and stealing the grass. #SometimesIChewOnHim #AndHeYells

30

Unfortunately, the week also brought a horrible no-good baff. I was mad, but I let Mommy hold me while I chewed on my new fren and figured out how to eat her face without causing squeaks. #IBitesBecauseILoves

I'm also enclosing videos and pictures from a walk one evening at dusk. Daddy says there is a big heron sitting just feet away from me that I didn't notice. And one up on the roof. #IDontBuyIt #ImABirdDogIWouldKnow

I insisted Karen join my on a walk one night this week. The hoomans fought me on this. Spoiler alert: I won.

I've also started implementing sit-in-refuse-to-budge tactics on our better walks. If I'm really feeling it and sense we are going to turn back towards home, I just refuse. I sit in the middle of the street refusing to move. Daddy argues with me and sometimes tries to beg me. It's cute. It usually ends in Daddy picking me up and carrying me. #Bonus

One not so great part of this week was bile-gate. I woke up at 6:27 a.m. and puked on Mommy, the bed and the carpet. All that came out was yellow bile, but I made it count. I stepped in it and got it all over me. Mommy has a sensitive sniffer, so she was especially happy. I guess as unfair punishment they withheld my food alllll day. I didn't get breakfast until after a vet appointment at 2 p.m. Outrageous! The vet appointment was fun, though!! My tummy was better by that evening, and all is well. #IllPullAnythingToGetAVetApptForLovins

That's all the news and #Finnanigans from this week. Over and out.

Special Report

May 16, 2020 ·

Be the ball. Beeeee the balllll!

Week One Hundred Fifteen

May 23, 2020 ·

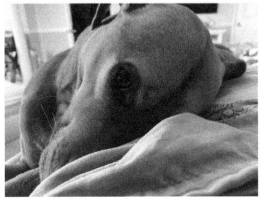

HI EVERYONE. FINN HERE with my week 115 report. I've recently negotiated 12.2 hours of mandatory daily nap time into my employment agreement. I'm taking this duty seriously. #SomebodyHasTo

The Squishy One and I got into a fight about bacon. I gave her my very bestest puppy dog eyes, pitiful eyes, and disappointed-in-you eyes. But she held strong. #IHateWhenSheHoldsStrong

It's been raining here so much. I don't like getting wet. I also don't like my raincoat. It's hard to know what to do. I tried to take Corporal Ducky outside for the pee-pee time but the Squishy One wouldn't let me. She said he can't get wet, and he will get smelly. Hello! He's a duck, you fool. He's waterproof. #ShesTheWorst

There's a new video on my FinnTube channel showing my hard work with Daddy this week on training. We focused on giving me treats when I go over and under his leg. We're building his calf muscles for faster walkies. And I get lots of treats each session. #ThatRightThereIsAWinWin

I got two great doses of neighbor-lovin's this week!! Finally, my adoring fans are back. First, Janice gave me lovin's and told me I'm adorable. Then I got to kiss all the Ellings and hear how charming and attractive I am. #TheyreSmartAndInsightfulHoomans

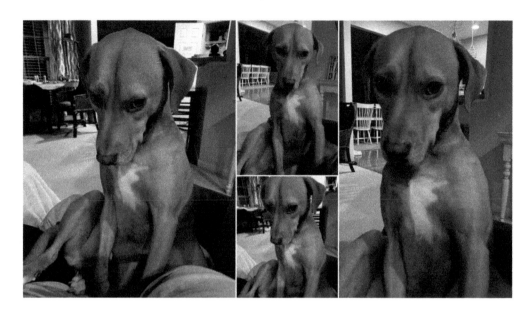

We saw Fergie during a walk later, and I tried to ask for her number. Our hoomans were all up in our business, so I couldn't talk to her alone. She tries to play it cool with me, but I think the chances she doesn't adore me are quite low. #LLFinn #ButImNotSureFergieDoes

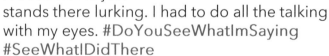

I had several one-on-one coaching sessions with the Squishy One this week about her attitude. She's not really been doing her best work lately, and it's affecting the whole team (really just me and the Kraken; Daddy is oblivious). The Kraken

didn't contribute much to the feedback. He just stands there lurking. I had to do all the talking with my eyes. #DoYouSeeWhatImSaying #SeeWhatIDidThere

That's all the news and #Finnanigans from this week. Over and out.

Week One Hundred Sixteen

May 30, 2020 ·

HI EVERYONE. FINN HERE with my week 116 report. Something is going on with Mommy's paw, and I don't like it. She screeches whenever I (we'll say, "accidentally") stand on it. Now she has some strange grey thing wrapped around it called "a splint." It prevents her from doing very important things related to my care and feeding, and that cannot stand. One-handed scratchies are woefully inadequate. And she's pretty slow on the blankie cover-me-up maneuvers now. #TwoStarsTops

I've been extra doting lately and also very curious about the splint. I sniff it methodically, up and down, inside and out at least three times a day to study its ways. I've also been laying across Mommy pretty much non-stop to halp her heal. #SmotheringIsMyLoveLanguage

Mommy opened up the pantry where we keep my food and the horrible-no good broom monster fell out and hit the floor. She jumped and squealed, and I jumped and squealed. This validated all my fears about the evil broom monster. I ran over to halp her by standing behind and between her legs quivering. #Brave Now I can't walk anywhere near that pantry or even that side of the kitchen. #ItsASituation #MyFoodIsTrappedInThereWithIt #SaveMyFood #FreeTheKibble

I've been in negotiations with the hoomans for some time about getting me a kitten. The Squishy One says she

is allergic (see also: whiner), so we can't have one. But I want one sooooo bad. There's a new video on FinnTube of our latest argument about this. Please go watch the video and leave reasons in the comments on FinnTube to halp me win my argument! #ItsNotFair

One great discovery this week is something the hoomans call an "eye mask." I don't know why they've been holding out on me until now. This magnificent device blocks the light from my eyes when I'm trying to sleep. I borrowed Mommy's satin eye mask and just loved it. I got a solid two hours of quality snoozle time. I've asked the Squishy One to get me one of my own. #IHopeItComesWithEarPlugsToo #TheyAreSoChatty

I got unfairly yelled at this week for a case of clear entrapment. The Hairy One left the can of pumpkin up on the counter and walked away. Clearly a signal to halp myself, I jumped up and tried to get some. But my tongue could barely reach, so I mostly just flicked pumpkin mush all over the counter. #HardlyWorthIt #INeedANewLawyer

I attended a virtual family brunch this morning with the hoomans. I got to meet my new cousin Clarence (he's a cute rescue, too), and MacKenzie had a pretty kitty I really wanted to taste. But they were all trapped inside the screen, so I couldn't even sniff or lick anyone. #Taunting

That's all the news and #Finnanigans from this week. Over and out.

Week One Hundred Seventeen

June 6, 2020 ·

HI EVERYONE. FINN HERE with my week 117 report. What a week! It's really been an emotional roller coaster.

First, we had some lovely deck time last Saturday and Sunday. I chose the Corporal for his first mission out on the deck. Other than his silence during obviously threatening bird-flyovers, he did great. I could have used some backup. Alas, he was a rock in the face of danger. #IJustNeedALittleMoreRoll

Daddy and I keep getting in trouble during staff meetings. He breathes weird or blinks funny (obviously instigating play), and I have to investigate by nibbling his face. Then he laughs and pushes me away. Then we wrastle. Then Mommy yells at us to focus. #ShesSoDemanding #WeAreFocusingJustNotOnHer

I told you last week that the hoomans took everything out of the pantry for no reason. Well, some new shelves came, and they put everything back. #ThankDog My OCD can't handle things out of place. But the Evil Broom Monster re-emerged strong and fierce for battle. The skirmish lastest over 7 minutes before it relented and crawled back into the pantry. There's an abridged video of the battle on my FinnTube channel. #VictoryIsMine

Speaking of the pantry, we also got in a new shipment of my new allergy kibble. Daddy says it's too expensive to waste, so he measures more carefully now. I supervised the transfer of said kibble from bag to bin and may have snuck a few pieces during careful inspection. #QualityControl #MicromanagingForTheBestResults

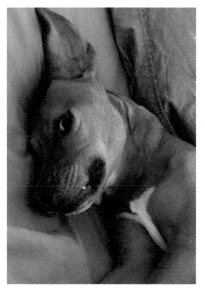

Mommy took this embarrassing picture of me during my nap. I'm furious. This is not my best side, and my snaggletooth is showing. #SheCantBeTrusted

Daycare was definitely the highlight of the week. The hoomans surprised me Wednesday with a whole day at daycare. So many of my friends were there, and we had so much fun. Within an hour I was muddy and hogging the little pool. But I did share when the other doggies asked to come in. #TheMuddierTheBetter

When I got home, we went for a nice walk then worked on some new training. The hoomans appeared to want me to lay on a new red cot. I wanted them to give me treats. I got 37 treats and laid on it only twice. #WhosTrainingWho #ExcellentRatio

That's all the news and #Finnanigans from this week. Over and out.

Week One Hundred Eighteen

June 13, 2020 ·

HI EVERYONE. FINN HERE with my week 118 report. We spent a few hours outside last Saturday. It was super-hot. The hoomans kept shooing me off their laps and trying to get me to lay on that new dog cot. I found this all incredibly rude and selfish. "It's too hot for a fur blanket, Finn." Well, it's never too hot to ignore your wishes and do what I want, hooman. These fools honestly think I'm going to downgrade from plush deck lounger at hooman level of prominence to small dog cot on the ground. I did walk near it and sniff it to give them false hope a few times. I love messing with them. #TheyreDelusional #CotWars #NoPawTouchedThatCot

I did, however, give in on the pool. I usually pretend I don't know what it is or how it works. Just to mess with them, mostly. I rather enjoy watching them splash, point, and carry on to try to get me in. Their voices get so high pitched. They're adorable. This time, they put little fake fish in there for me to play with. They were fun and intriguing. Apparently, "play with" didn't mean cronch. #ButILikeCronch

Okay, quick update on the cot situation. During day two of the cot wars, I caved. They refused me access to their thrones, so I had no choice. I certainly wasn't going to lay on the ground. I at least held out until I was given a cushion like they have. #TheyWinThisRound

The highlight of the week was receiving another goody package from Aunt Susan! This one had an octopus fren exactly the size of my mouf. I've been carrying him everywhere, and the Squishy One laughs like an idiot when I prance down the hallway with just the legs dangling out of my mouf... dancing against my face as I prance. I named him Frank and immediately got to work on amputating one of his legs. He's a septopus now.
#HeDidntNeedItAnyway
#DontBeAComplainerFrank

My custom eye masks arrived and I love them. I'm working on ways to tell Mommy I need one placed on my face. She doesn't always pay attention and sometimes I have to nap with the light in my eyes. #Slacker

I feel very powerful in my dragon mask and feel it will ward off enemies while I sleep. #Fierce #Dragginator

Mommy likes the shark mask the best because she says it's like a warning label to others about me. #NoBites #MustBite

June 12th was the 2nd anniversary since I signed the adoption papers for these two freaks. It's hard to believe I've been molding their little hearts and minds for two years. #AndTheyreVeryLittle

That's all the news and #Finnanigans from this week. Over and out.

Week One Hundred Nineteen

June 20, 2020 ·

HI EVERYONE. FINN HERE with my week 119 report. The hoomans and I went for a wonderful ride last Sunday. It's was Mommy's first time in a car or away from the house in 92 days. She really needed the adventure! #WeAllDid

We drove with the windows down, smelling all the smells. We went to a magical land called Assateague Island where Mommy said something called "wild ponies" live and play. We drove through really slowly with the windows cracked looking for these mysterious creatures. I stood on Mommy's lap for the whole drive around the ponies' park. She loved it. Every so often she'd ask me to get off her face so she could breathe. #ShesSoNeedy #Whiner

The poop smells were uhhhmazing. Sometimes we'd pass a huge pile of steaming poop on the side of the road, and I would try to climb out the window to go roll in it. There were even Finn-sized mounds of poop calling my name. But the Squishy One kept pulling me back. #Rude #PoopIsLife

We finally came upon some of these "wild ponies." Apparently, "wild ponies" is what these idiots call gigantic danger-dogs. They were the biggest dogs I've ever seen. They had very long snouts with big eyes and feet. They were clearly a threat! I bravely barked and cried a lot when they were too close to the car. #ItWasANightMare #IHadAFoalProofPlan #ISavedThemAgain

We drove along the ocean on the way home and saw so many beach chickens screaming, "mine, mine" as they swooped down and snatched things off the ground. They're just lucky I wasn't on the beach to catch them! #IllBeBack

I also got a day at daycare with my number-one girlfriend, Jessica. It was awesome. I chased around a puppy German Shepard named Sadie all morning and rough-housed with my buddy Grover in the mud all afternoon. I was gloriously filthy. #MudLife #GroverSmilesALot

Jess caught an unfortunate moment of bad behavior on video. She was coming to the gate and I didn't want Grover to get a drop of her attention, so I shoved his big goofy head away. I had

to claim Jess for my own. Well, I guess Jess didn't like that because then she betrayed me with a baff! I was delightfully filthy, and she ruined it. #IWasWronged #WhyYouDoMeLikeThatJess

When Daddy brought me home, I ran to Mommy and made her swaddle me in a blanket while I quivered and told her about the horrible baff betrayal. While I was trapped in her love-swaddle, she lectured me about playing nice with Grover. #YadaYadaYada #BlahBlahBlah #IDoWhatIWant

We are still having lots of fun with Frank. I have no idea how it happened, but he's down another dangly bit, so Mommy says he's a sextopus now.
#ThenThereWereSix

After weeks of telepathically communicating my need for watermelon, the hoomans finally got it! I love the watermelon. Nom Nom Nom. I'm now focusing my transmissions on frozen dairy slop.
#DairyQueenComeSaveMe

That's all the news and #Finnanigans from this week. Over and out.

Special Report

June 23, 2020 ·

I'm in charge of all package inspection around here.

Week One Hundred Twenty

June 27, 2020 ·

HI EVERYONE. FINN HERE with my week 120 report. It's been a leisurely week here at Chateau du Finnegan. We spent Sunday celebrating the "Father's Day" holiday dedicated to the great and powerful Hairy One. Mommy says there is a whole holiday dedicated to him... as it should be. I gave him Me-themed prezzies (a puzzle with my gorgeous face on it, a printed picture of us kissing and holding paws in the grass, and a deck of playing cards with a picture of us having bro time on the boardwalk last year.) #ImAGiftEveryday #HesALuckyFather

The Squishy One is coming along nicely in her training lately. She made me not one, but two snow cone treats this week. Just surprised me, mid-day, for no reason. She crushes up the good ice into mush for me then adds flavors. One day it was the water left over from boiling chicken and a couple days later it was watermelon mush! I even got Daddy to spoon feed me the watermelon one. #TrainerLevelNinja #ItsGoodToBeKing

Captain Ducky had a harrowing mission this week that left him at half weight and down one wing. He's currently waiting at Urgent Care in the spare closet. The wait time has been ridiculous. I've demanded to see a supervisor, but she keeps rolling her eyes at me and walking away. Corporal Ducky is having some shell shock from seeing the skirmish. The enemy was relentless in their disemboweling. #TheyHaveYetToBeIdentified #ThatsGonnaNeedStitches

While the Captain is stuck in the throes of the healthcare system and the Corporal just lays there staring off into space, I've been spending more time with Karen the Funky Rubber Chicken. We call her Karen for short. Daddy even let me take her on some walks this week. #SheLovedIt

I've identified an important new sound for the K9 Academy library audio-archives. Every dog should be taught to identify this sound as early as possible in life. Egg shells cracking open!! It's hard to hear from across the house, but I can tune in now at the first crrrrrackle and appear at Mommy's side almost instantly as she peels the hardboiled eggies. It's important to effectively communicate that I want some. I'm partial to the yellow center and she's partial to the white part. Really, I'm partial to all of it, but she won't share the white part. #SelfishMuch

I had some nice play time with the hoomans this morning. Every 6th and 7th day they seem to sleep in, linger around in their sleeping platform, and cuddle. It's my favorite time. We play, I bites, Daddy says, "No bites!" and I laugh and bites again. I get a toy and bring it to him for play, and he pretends he doesn't want it, but we all know he does. Mommy drinks her nasty hot brown water and watches me and Daddy wrastle. I like 6th and 7th days. #WeShouldNameThemSomething

That's all the news and #Finnanigans from this week. Over and out.

Week One Hundred Twenty-One

July 4, 2020 ·

HI EVERYONE. FINN HERE with my week 121 report. Quick question: What does the Squishy One mean when she says, "I think we should get a young female rescue next? Ya know, so he has a friend, and I have someone to put dresses on." I heard her say it on the phone to someone. I'm at a loss why we would need a second rescuer around here. I'm doing JUST FINE managing this household on my own. Who does she think she is!?! Thank DOG Daddy seems to be holding the line.

#AlthoughAnAssistantManagerMightBeFunToBossAround

I've made great progress grooming Frank this week. Mommy keeps taking him away and saying, "Frank is friend not food." Yeah, yeah, woman. He likes it. I've gotten half his tentacles off now. Soon he will be just be a ball. <insert evil laughter> #AndThenThereWereFour

Daddy betrayed me and Karen this week. I entrusted her to Mommy's care when we fell asleep (she's the night nanny), when all of a sudden I was startled awake by Karen's rubber chicken screams. I found Daddy holding her by the neck and looking guilty. I rescued Karen from his

clutches and gave him the stink eye the rest of the night.
#ThisIsWhyIHaveTrustIssues
#SomeNannyShels

I enjoyed a couple good Kong's this week on my new throne (cot). I've accepted they won the last round of #CotWars, but I've also decided to snatch victory from the paws of defeat. I've been experimenting with getting on the cot when it's parked inside the house and when they haven't asked me to. This seems to amuse them and sometimes results in treats. It also shows I'm in charge and I'll do what I want. It's unclear why and results are inconsistent, but I will keep at it. #IMostlyStillActLikeItsLavaWhenWereOutside

The hoomans claim today is their 21st wedding anniversary. (I've seen no evidence to substantiate this.) It's also Mr. Snuggles' 17th birthday, his third

at the rainbow bridge. I think I'll pick out one of his old toys and disembowel it in his honor, today. Usually, the hoomans go watch boom popper anxiety makers on their anniversary. But they said this year we are going to stay home and watch a movie. We watched something this week that didn't end well for the horse. I hope tonight's selection is better!
#IHopeTheresAStrongCanineLead

That's all the news and #Finnanigans from this week. Over and out.

Week One Hundred Twenty-Two

July 11, 2020 ·

HI EVERYONE. FINN HERE with my week 122 report. It's been a banner week here at House of Finn. The Squishy One fiiiiinally got my book done and published for the world to see. #TookHerLongEnough This is step one in my journey to world domination. #StepTwoIsEllenDeGeneres

Thanks to all of my adoring fans and let's be honest, my stunning face on the cover, the rush of pre-orders skyrocketed the book to #1 on Amazon's Hot New Releases, and we even beat out Garfield!!! Any day I triumph over a cat is a good day. All that's left is for my attorney, Bert, to negotiate me a stellar contract. I'm hoping for a 100% dollar-to-bone conversion agreement. #IDeserveIt

The Squishy One and I are working on book two now. She says it needs editing, and I say my original words are perfect just the way they are. #HowCanYouEditPerfection

Last weekend the Hairy One decided we should celebrate the hoomans' 21st wedding anniversary with a movie outside on the deck. We watched him set up a big screen and fuss with a projector and sound bar for an hour – all so we could sit in the suffocating humidity to watch more yacking hoomans. #HesATrooper #WhyThough #WeHaveSofasInside

It was also the 4th of July, so the occasional backyard firework went off. Why these fools wanted to sit outside in a war zone was beyond me. I splayed myself across Mommy to protect her from fireworks shrapnel and errant bugs. We snuggled under the blanket, and I gave Daddy side eye for making us sit out here like wild animals. #ImMoreOfACentralACDog

I also got playcare time this week with my #1 girlfriend Jessica, my buddy Jameson and a new frenemy named Mila. Jess texted the Squishy One pictures and videos of my day. First, I stole Mila's kennel and found it super irritating when she came by to ask when she could have it back. Then I rode Jameson around the yard a while and generally threw attitude and sass at Jess. #SideEyeIsAnExpressionOfLove #ItsGoodToKeepHerOnHerToes

I decided to celebrate myself with some me-time. So I enjoyed a playcare spa mud treatment and a mani/pedi. No one was available to give me a seaweed wrap, and I didn't get any cucumber slices for my eyes or a single glass of blackberry ginger white rhino breath citrus healing hydration tonic. #WhatKindOfSpaIsThis #TwoStars

The hoomans left me unattended for two hours one evening, and I was livid. I spent the time amputating tree frog's right arm and then left it on the Squishy One's pillow as a warning. #CouldntFindAHorseHead

Frank's fourth arm has mysteriously vanished and now he is a triopus. In shocking and unrelated news, one of Frank's tentacles came out in my poop!! The Hairy One got all excited and then stole it to show the Squishy One. #IWasSavingThatForLater #AndThenThereWereThree

We woke up Friday to brown stuff on the ceiling in the bedroom. I thought it looked fine, a nice touch of poopy brown rococo period accent for an otherwise boring white ceiling. But the hoomans did not agree. I had to spend time in the fortress of solitude while the hoomans ran around moving furniture and carrying on about this "roof leak." #GoAwayFay #TheseFreaksNameStorms

The new furniture arrangement has my OCD pinging off the charts. Nothing is where it's supposed to be. It's utter chaos. At one point, my bed was actually TOUCHING the dresser foot and on the other side of the room!!!
THE OTHER SIDE OF THE ROOM.

I knew I couldn't live like this. I cried until Daddy moved my bed back to at least the right side of the room, even if it's not in the agreed upon placement exactly 2.678 feet from the window wall and 6.1263749 feet from the desk wall. #ImNothingIfNotFlexible

I spent some time during the storm monitoring a family of ducks in the pond across the lane. I found their behavior confusing and potentially delicious. I know from K9 Academy training and of course, Caddyshack, that in order to catch the duck, I have to become the duck. #QuackQuack #IMakeAHandsomeDuck #TheyllNeverSeeMeComing

I think I'm especially adorable in this video and these pics of my playtime with Karen the rubber chicken and that everyone at the academy should get to see them. #Generous

That's all the news and #Finnanigans from this week. Over and out.

Week One Hundred Twenty-Three

July 18, 2020 ·

HI EVERYONE. FINN HERE with my week 123 report. The Squishy One has one job, ok maybe two. But one of those is wiping away my eye-boogies. I like that done within 37-42.5 seconds of waking up. Lately she's been really slacking on this. I try to climb on her chest while she's still sleeping to alert her. But she just yelps. #ICanPoopInYourShoeAnytimeIWant

Ooooh.... ants! On Sunday morning I heard the Squishy One stumble to the kitchen to make her nasty brown water. Then I heard her scream, "Evvvvvvvvvvvannnnnn!!!!" That's what she calls the Hairy One when he's in trouble or she is. We rushed in to see what was wrong and saw Ant-Maggedon. It was glorious. Those little guys were scurrying everywhere and very focused on their parade. I tried to halp, and the Squishy One dragged me away to let Daddy save us all. I don't know what the big deal was. They looked fun. Mommy freaked out and took everything out of the kitchen to wash. She muttered a lot and seemed more nutso than usual. #AndThatsSayingSomething #ThenThereWasBleach #SoMuchBleach

On Tuesday, the nice men came to work on our leaky roof. So I got to go to playcare. THERE WAS A PUPPY!! She was so fluffy and soft. I took care of her all day and made sure she wasn't scared. The hoomans called her Koa but I called her Mine-O-Mine. She obviously

looked up to me for my rugged good looks and devilish charm. #WhoWouldnt #LLFinn

The Squishy One put this absurd hat on me and made me look at her for a picture. She claims it "just came in the mail" and has no idea how it all happened. The indignity I suffer is real. Then she did it to Corporal Ducky! #ImAnInternationallyCelebratedAuthorDangIt #OKThatMightBeAStretch

The Squishy One has been hearing from more and more Finn fans lately, and I love it when she reads me their messages. She says I shouldn't let it go to my head. Spoiler Alert: too late.

She said Jenni's husband, Jay, the Head Ginger in Charge #HGIC at Jenni's house, is a big fan even though he's not on Facebook to tell me himself. #TwoPointsDeducted #HiJay

Mommy just asked me if I'm ready for a baff. SHE IS THE WORST. Why does she do this to me?! I hate baffs so much. #NegativeGhostRiderThePatternIsFull

That's all the news and #Finnanigans from this week. Over and out.

Week One Hundred Twenty-Four

July 25, 2020 ·

HI EVERYONE. FINN HERE with my week 124 report. Daddy has been pushing back lately on my entirely normal and incessant demand for hunts. I've trained him that some walks are for checking peemail (sniffing messages and leaving replies) and some are for hunting jumpies and snails. Hunting walks go very very slowly and he gets antsy. So, I staged a sit-in when he tried to drag me home prematurely the other day. He texted the Squishy One, and then I had to listen to her drone on about respecting Daddy's wishes and how it's too hot for hunting walks. #WhatAWhiner #SnitchesGetStitches

I got to see my #1 girlfriend, Jess, on Wednesday. What a rush! I forgot we had a date and lost my mind when I saw her pull up. Mommy was a little jealous because I jumped in Jess's Jeep without so much as a look back. #SmellYaLata #GottaRide

Jess took me to daycare so she could show me off to the other dogs. We had a great time and even posed for prom portraits. #SheCantQuitMe I also spent time teaching our new friend, Yonya, that I require all the attention at all times. #ThisLapIsntBigEnoughForBothOfUs

I've given in entirely on the #CotWars now. The Squishy One strategically places it in sunbeams inside the house. And I can't resist. #SunDog

I had some nice playtime with Daddy one morning on the big bed. Mommy woke up startled and yelped at us. There was some unnecessary name calling, but then she started recording!

This may or may not have been the morning after I kept everyone up until 2:30 playing with my loudest toys. #KarenTheRubberChicken #ForTheWin

I could tell Mommy was jealous, so I gave her some one-on-one snuggle time. She put on the Dish Network Heartland Dishscape channel for me. We heard horses, chickens, and dogs barking. Sometimes a truck drove by. Then there were carnival sounds and fireflies. It was soothing until we heard something called a rooster. It was screaming, so I started huffing and chuffing to warn it away. I saved us. Again. #RoostersSoundDelicious #AHerosWorkIsNeverDone

On Friday I decided to take Larry the Lobster along on our evening paramble. I showed him my favorite things and showed him off to everyone we passed. #AGoodTimeWasHadByAll #ExceptEveryoneJealousOfMyLarry

We love seeing all the #ImWithFinn hashtag challenge pictures you guys are posting with your copy of the book!! Keep it up!! #YoureTheBestPackAGuyCouldAskFor

That's all the news and #Finnanigans from this week. Over and out.

Special Report
July 29, 2020 ·

I am embracing my Viking power. What should my Viking name be?

Finn the Impaler? Finn the Screamer?

Week One Hundred Twenty-Five

August 1, 2020 ·

HI EVERYONE. FINN HERE with my week 125 report. We had a pretty fun week here at the ranch. Ok, there's no cattle here but I wish there were. Mommy insisted on making some dumb video for the "tell your dog a story" challenge. That involved her making a series of concrete and contractually-obligating offers about treats, go-for-a-rides, camp, and squirrels. I was furious when it was clear litigation would be necessary to make her pay up. #CallMeForProBONEOHours

Daddy paid her bill by taking me to the stinky bay for a quick walk in the smelly water and sand. I found a dead monster Daddy called a horseshoe crab.

#ItLookedNothingLikeAShoeOrACrab I love the smell of rotting seafood. #TheDeaderTheBetter

Later in the week she recorded me lovingly grooming Larry the Lobster. When I noticed this intrusion of privacy, I told her to knock it off. She lied to my face and pretended she wasn't recording. #ShesAnIdiot

The Squishy One has taken to ordering stoopid hats for me lately. I didn't understand why at first and threw her lots of shade during "just look at me and smile, Finn" pictures. My main goal during these sessions is to not smile or look at her so she plies me with treats in her ever quest for one good picture with my ears up. #MaybeAnotherTreatWouldHalp

But this week's hat was different. It started out the same... salty glares at her camera, then treats, then more salty glares. But that was only until Daddy showed me a historical documentary called "What's Opera, Doc?" by a famous warrior called Bugs Bunny. (Again, with the hooman naming of things.... I saw no bugs.) Anyway, this showed me how powerful and mighty my new Viking Hat really was. I felt all my Viking power surge through me and we went hunting wabbits. #ImNowToBeReferredToAsFinnTheImpaler #KillTheWabbitKillTheWabbit

Last night was stressful. I discovered two holes in the ceiling of the bedroom that seemed an obvious danger. I sat under the holes for an hour to make sure nothing planned to exit them. When I decided it was safe, I went to lay down in my bed and found it perched up on a pile of furniture in the corner of the room. But, I'm a problem solver. The hoomans aren't sure how I managed to get up there and balance just right without tumbling over. #CuzImAVikingThatsHow

That's all the news and #Finnanigans from this week. Over and out.

Special Report

August 6, 2020 ·

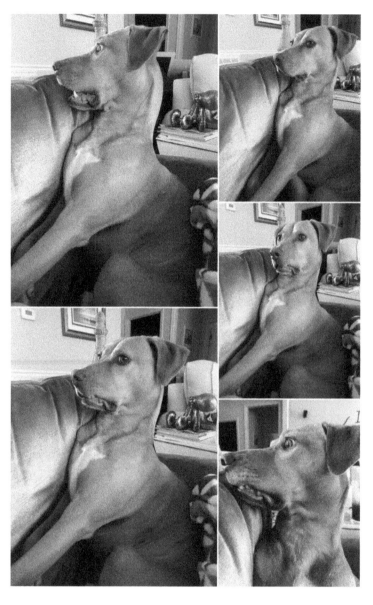

The phases of dwerp when you've been sleeping on the job and think you hear a squirrel. Then side-eye Mommy like it's her fault there's no one there. #Suspicious

Week One Hundred Twenty-Six
August 8, 2020 ·

HI EVERYONE. FINN HERE with my week 126 report. In celebration of the book release, I ordered myself some new race car jammies. They make me dream of go-for-rides to the park. It's been hard work, and I deserve some pampering. #MyLifeIsSoCalgon

The Squishy One has been so annoying about pawtographing and shipping the special signed books. She wants me over there halping all the time. #HelloIHavePeopleForThat #ImUpperManagement

And she keeps rustling tissue paper over there. Tissue paper is what my Santa Paws and birthday prezzies are wrapped in. I can't halp myself when I hear it. I've charged her a few times and get pushed away. #UntilSheWantsMyPawPrintAgain

We had a nasty storm on Tuesday that brought down some trees in our neighborhood. I posed in front of one and pretended I toppled it down to get to a bird. The hoomans laughed and laughed. #OkSoDidI #BirdDogJokes

The hoomans have been throwing around "good boy" a lot lately and treats don't follow. When a hooman says "good boy," a dog gets a treat. Period. This is a widely-known unspoken contractual arrangement. The Squishy One has been all over me to heel on our walks, but she's stingy with the treats. I've taken to jamming my snout into Mommy's hand as we

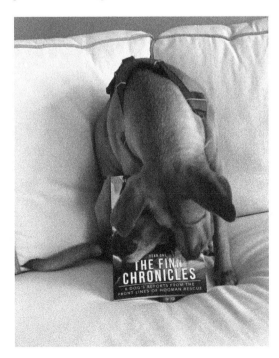

walk to remind her where to put them. Even that doesn't work. She is infuriating. #NoTreatNoHeelWoman

I got to go to daycare again this week while the hoomans painted the ceiling. I JUST got used to the new furniture arrangement (piled against a wall), and now they move it back again. It's chaos here. I hope this brings #RoofLeak2020 to a close. #MakeItStop

 Paws down, the best news of the week was our surprise prezzie from Julie! Mommy has known Julie since they were puppies at their hooman academy. Julie used a photo to make the most amazing drawing of me. There's even a video of it as she progresses through the drawing. It's neat and everyone should watch it! I can't wait to see it hanging in our house for everyone to admire. #BowBeforeMe #TheBiggerTheBetter #MaybeItShouldReplaceTheTV

That's all the news and #Finnanigans from this week. Over and out.

Special Report

August 10, 2020 ·

I'm feeling better, but still milking another sick day out of this. Just watching a little TV with my Squishy One. Feeling cute... might build a blanket fort later.

Week One Hundred Twenty-Seven

August 15, 2020 ·

HI EVERYONE. FINN HERE with my week 127 report. What a great week!!!!! Right after I posted my last update, the hoomans said, "Go for a ride," and off we went on a long day of adventures. #ILoveAdventures #WeHaventHadAdventuresForMonths

We started at the frozen dairy slop dispensary. A nice lady there gave me tastes of all the ice cream flavors on cute little spoons. I guess these are the perks of being a huge local celebrity? #ImFamousNow I even got her to let me try the bacon one twice. TWICE!!! #LLFinn I settled on the cheese ice cream with dried liver and tripe sprinkles. It was delicious! Daddy held it for me so I could get maximum tongue to ice cream contact. #FinallyTheServiceIDeserve #ItsAboutTime

Then we went to a new little town I've never peed in called Lewes. Daddy went into a bookstore and talked to the nice lady who came outside to fuss over me and told me I'm the cutest author she's ever met. #OrWillEverMeetIAssureYou #BiblionBooks

We wandered into a little store full of dog things. There, a nice lady found out I was a rescue and tied a bright red bandana on me. To thank her, I jumped up on the counter and pulled down lots of stuff that made loud noises when it fell. While Daddy was trying to pick it up, I jumped on his head and knocked him over. We all had a blast. #YoureWelcome #ImAFurryMayhemCommercial

Then, we went to Patti and Richie's house and met their new puppy, Stella. She was so dreamy and beautiful. I was extra sweet to her and mostly respected her boundaries. #HeavyOnTheMostly She's still a little afraid of new hoomans and dogs. I was the goodest boy. #Stellllllluhhhhhh #FutureGirlfriend

Then we drove a long time to a wonderful place called Greyhound Bookstore & Fine Art. Mommy went inside and talked to a nice lady about selling my book, and she said yes!! They asked me to come inside to give me treats and take a picture of me with my book.
#FinallySomeoneWhoUnderstandsImTheAuthorNotHer But, I got so excited I peed on their beautiful historic wood floors. While Mommy was trying to clean that up (and shooting me an epic evil eye), I jumped up on the edge of a table to get a closer look at this "fine art." Mommy saw me and gasped, then Daddy dove on me to pull me back before the table fell over. I bring excitement and fun everywhere I go. #YoureWelcome The nice man there gave me treats and I peed again. #IWasMemorableAtLeast

The next day I woke up with super goopy eyes. Mommy cleaned them, and they just filled with more goop. She refused to let me eat any of it despite my best killer shark moves. #Outrageous This went on all day. I like to schedule all my illnesses on Sundays when the vet is closed. #ThenItsHerProblem Dr.

Mommy thought it was allergies from our adventures the day before. I made her hold me in her arms all day. #SickDay #HerDegreeIsFromWebMD

I picked my pupsicle jammies for bed that night and crashed early. I woke up pretty early and surprised Mommy by jumping on her face to kiss her awake. #SheLovesItSoMuchSheScreams #HoldStillLetMeLoveYou

I told her I still wasn't feeling well even though the goop was mostly gone. We agreed I needed another sick day in bed. So, I put on my Viking hat and we watched some TV. She put on Animal Planet and we learned about otters and tigers. They both looked like they'd be fun to play with. #HereKittyKitty I asked if we could build a blanket fort and nap inside but she said no. #ShesAJerk

let's play
SUSPICIOUS OR
DELICIOUS?

@FINNCHRONICLES

On Wednesday we spent some time playing a new game I call: suspicious or delicious? The front window gives me a Finn's eye view of the community pool and club house. I can watch all the hoomans and littles walking to and from the pool with all their bits. Floaty bits, towels, coolers, toys, and other fun-looking accessories. Mommy and I watch each gaggle and decide if they look suspicious or delicious. Spoiler alert: everyone looks delicious. #CantHoldMyLicker #ComeHereAndLetMeLickYourFaceOff

Tell HQ treat supply room to stock up on Himalayan Dog Chews. #HardCheeseIsDelicious

That's all the news and #Finnanigans from this week. Over and out.

Week One Hundred Twenty-Eight

August 22, 2020 ·

HI EVERYONE. FINN HERE with my week 128 report. It was a fairly boring week here at Castle du Finnegan until this morning. More on that later. #ThereWasCussingAgain

The battles about midnight walks continue with the Hairy One. He's back sliding in his training and it's exhausting. The first few steps are the same: I smack Mommy with my paw until she wakes up and tells Daddy I need to pee (aka hunt snails). He grumbles and stumbles around getting dressed (unnecessary step I'd like to eliminate from the process). He looks me dead in the eye and says, "Finn, we're just going potty. No hunting, and don't eat off the ground." #OkBuddyYouBetcha I roll my eyes so hard they could pop out. We go outside, and I immediately start hunting and trying to eat the teeny snails. He dental-dives and steals them right out of my mouf! We continue. I bark and carry on as loudly as possible so I can hear the beautiful echoes of myself ricochet around the still neighborhood and let people know I'm coming. #PaulRevereStyle He gets mad and tells me to stop it. #HesJealousOfMyGifts Then -- and this is where things have been falling apart lately -- he gets super mad and carries me home! #Unacceptable #ThoseSnailsArentGonnaHuntThemselvesYouFool

I got to go to daycare on Monday. It was so great. I played and wrastled all day. Me and the guys had fun carrying on. That is, until Mommy decided I needed a horrible no good awful baff. She said I stunk and my shedding was making her crazy. First of all, I smelled delicious. Like a combination of salty Fritos mixed with grass clippings and dirt. It takes time and strategy to develop just the right funk. #ACertainJeNeSaisQuoi Second, she whines and whines about my delightful hair tickling her nose and ending up in her food like it's a bad thing. #ShedHappens #ItsCalledFinnFettiCuzItsFun

After the awful baff, Mommy swaddled me in dryer-heated towels so I wouldn't die. Mommy heats my towels in the dryer for the post-baff shiver-quiver-recovery wrap in her arms. I cry and carry on, and she holds me in clouds of warm fluffy towels until I fall asleep. Mommy says I'm a spoiled dog. #TheresNoSuchThing

Mommy has started giving me local raw honey to halp me with my allergies. She's mixing it in yogurt and I'm loving it! Daddy tries to halp me by holding the spoon and I lick so aggressively that he drops it and flings sticky yogurt everywhere. #ImAnAggressiveLicker

We've had so much rain this week. I can't stand peeing in the rain, and forget pooping. #NotGonnaHappen #YouGottaKnowWhenToHoldEm

The hoomans have also started up again with the dreaded teefs brushing. What a fight. How can they expect me not to cronch down on the brush?! #CronchIsLife #SometimesItsAFingerThough #ThenTheresYelping

So... about the excitement this morning. Daddy and I went for our normal Saturday morning patrol of the 'hood. I scarfed something up and had it in my mouf before Daddy could stop me. He took it out and stole it, like usual, but then he got very upset. He said now I'd really done it - gotten hold of a mushroom. We ran home for Mommy to halp and she called poison control

while Daddy went back to bag up the blob of white something he'd removed from my mouf and thrown aside. I hear Mommy talking about how to make me barf (which, for the record, is usually frowned on around here). Then, just after Mommy gave the nice man her money number, Daddy runs in with the evidence baggie. Then I heard her say, "Wait... this is a French fry or something." After a brief relief-laugh, things got heavy and they had a long talk with me about eating stuff off the ground. Daddy said we're going to "redouble our efforts."
#WhatDoesThatEvenMean and the awful Hannibal Lecter mask is coming back for our walks. #HelloClarice #ImmaFightYouOnThis

That's all the news and #Finnanigans from this week. Over and out.

Special Report
August 23, 2020

Someone save me from these insufferable hooman servants.
#ImAFiveStarDogLivingInATwoStarHouse

Week One Hundred Twenty-Nine

August 29, 2020 ·

HI EVERYONE. FINN HERE with my week 129 report. I received three exciting prezzies this week. Those were definitely the highlight!! #ILovePrezzies

Fairy Godmother Julie sent me a gorgeous drawing of myself that Daddy hung on the wall for all to celebrate. It's high enough that I'm looking down on everyone. #AsItShouldBe #BowBeforeMeHoomans

I also got a new collar that's navy blue with anchors. I've never tried sailing but I think I'd be an excellent Captain. Don't I look dapper? #AuthoritySuitsMe

I also got some rather exciting news. Apparently, I'm so adorable and dashing that a bone-a-fide #GetIt bestselling author of cozy mystery books has put me on two of her book covers!!

This is the kind of appreciation and adoration I expect. #WellDoneMelissaBourbon I guess you could say I'm her dog-muse. #ImABigDeal #ImTheHandsomest #LetsAddCoverModelToMyResume

I've been taking Larry with me on walks lately. He seems to like the feeling of grass tickling his claws. #WhoDoesntThough #MindMeld

I pitifulled my way into some yogurt yesterday. But I only got to lick the scraps from the end of the container. Why don't I get full spoonfuls of yogurt like a king? Why am I treated with such disrespect? #Unacceptable #WheresMyFrozenDairySlop #ThereWillBeConsequencesLater

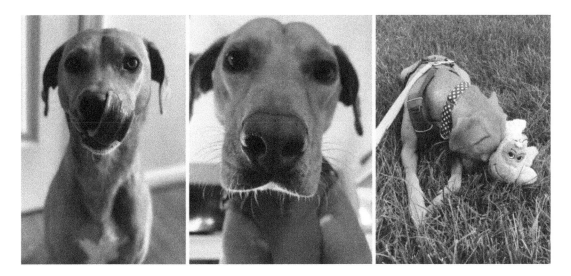

That's all the news and #Finnanigans from this week. Over and out.

Week One Hundred Thirty

September 5, 2020 ·

HI EVERYONE. FINN HERE with my week 130 report. What a week! It's been nonstop fun and excitement around here!! #ThanksToMeMostly

On Saturday we went back up to Lewes to check on the things I peed on a few weeks ago and to drop off some books at Biblion Bookstore. The nice lady there came out and gave me a treat!! She's selling my book there and said I'm adorable. #ShesSoRight

We stopped in Rehoboth on the way home for some sniffs. I didn't catch their names, but two pretty girls noticed me and ran directly over to fawn over me. #AsItShouldBe #LLFinn They squatted down and loved on me for a few minutes. They tasted delicious and told me I'm the handsomest. #TheySquealed #ISquealed

One saw the book in Mommy's hand and said "he's famous" and I realized something. I AM famous now. I need to start demanding new bonuses and luxuries commensurate with my stature. #MoreTreats #StatueAtHQPlease #WhenDoIGetMyKeyToTheExecutiveGrassPatch

We came home and the Squishy One gave me a new toy. This was a banner day. It was a red and orange octopus I named Steve. We played a long time! But I had already decided (during my "famousness revelation") that I wanted to see Dr. Richards and some vet techs who tell me I'm the cutest. #IWasOverdueForTheirAttention So, I set my plan in motion. I emptied my whole bladder on the living room floor. This usually gets me fast-tracked to the vet for some attention. Unsure if that was a one-off, the hoomans decided to take a wait-

and-see approach. #PeeHappens #NotByAccidentThough

Clearly, they weren't catching my drift. So about 90 minutes later I did it again. But this time I got to point two birds with one paw. The Hairy One gave me an awful-no-good baff, so I waited until it was over and I was all fluffy and clean. Then I let 'er rip all over him and the baffroom floor. #FeltSoGood

I decided I needed one more compelling symptom and I knew just the sucker to work-over. I ran to Mommy, cold and damp from that awful baff. I crawled into her lap, sad and dejected. Then I started to shake. Not a little shake. A full-blown eyebrow-to-tail quiver, like I could maybe be dying. She swaddled me up in the towels hot from the dryer and comforted me while she tried to figure out the problem. #IRequirePreheatedTowelsThanksVeryMuch #NowWhosWaitingAndSeeing

The plan worked. Kinda. Daddy took me to a vet, but it wasn't Dr R. It was something called a "much more expensive ER vet, why do you always do this on weekends, Finn?" #CuzICan #IOwnYou

It. Was. Awesome. Everyone loved me there, and we had 3 hours of crazy fun!! I got a full body massage from the doc, attention from all the techs and even some new procedures. Ultrasound? Yes, please, sounds fun. Oh, that belly massage with the little wand feels good. #WhereAreYouGoingDontStop X-ray? Sure, why not? I'm not buyin'. Can I lick you while we wait? Urinalysis with a machine read and a manual one? YOU BETCHA. #WhatElseYaGot #MaybeWeShouldDoThePhysicalAgain

After a while, I heard the doc call Mommy and say the only thing wrong with me was a "high pH," (I assume that means Pretty Handsome,) and also maybe "attentionitis". It was almost midnight by then, and Daddy was super happy to make the hour drive back home. #HeWasCrabby #NoTellingWhyThough #MustveBeenSomethingMommyDid

Fast forward to Friday, and we had ALL THE FUN. Daddy and Mommy got me dressed up, and we went out to get the Coastal Point newspaper fresh off the stands. #IHalped

Daddy and I sat down on a bench at the park so he could read me an article. And guys... IT WAS ABOUT ME. My picture was even in there. I could hardly believe it. #NowImEvenFamouser #IMadeHimReadItToMeTwice

That afternoon, I finally got to see Dr. Richards, too! And my #1 girlfriend Jess was even my tech. The plan had finally come full circle! I screamed and howled in the car until Jess came to get me. Another dog got to go in before me, and I freaked out at the indignity. #ImACount #WhatIsHe

Once inside, I cried and carried on if no one was loving on me. Then I got Jess to let me sit on her lap for the exam. I got a massage exam again, they stole my pee again, and Dr. Richards called my Mommy and said I was an angel. And after all that, my plan worked even better than I'd imagined. It turns out I have an actual UTI. A pretty good one, too! #ExtraCreditForMe I'm so glad that it was too soon for the ER Vet to see it so I could still go see Jess and Dr. Richards. #ImWinningAtLife

This week's well-spent vet bills: $927.63 #WorthIt

That's all the news and #Finnanigans from this week. Over and out.

Week One Hundred Thirty-One

September 12, 2020 ·

HI EVERYONE. FINN HERE with my week 131 report. It's been many nighnighs since I've seen my bacon dealer, Tony. I miss the smells of Turtle Beach Cafe and our nice walks on the boards. Daddy says now that it's second season and the crowds are gone, we can start walking in the boardwalk again and go see Tony soon. #TeamTony #BaconMan #SecondSeasonRocks

The COVID quarantine is starting to get to me. I accidentally took out my frustration on Frank and removed his final dangling leg thing. #RestInPiecesFrank

I've decided to up my vet-attention game with new food allergies. This has scored me an appointment with Dr. Jeffers next week! I can't wait. I hope we can have a rematch with the Qtips! #HesSoFast #CheatingOnDrRichardsAndDrK

It's also been many many nighnighs since I've been to the primary dwelling. We came back last night and it was glorious! I ran through the house checking every nook and cranny. I flung my toy basket into the air and inspected every squeaky, soft, hard, shiny and squishy thing. I jumped and rolled on every bed. And I squealed and cried with joy and zoomies. #AGoodTimeWasHadByAll

I woke Mommy up early this morning to tell her, "Happy Birthday." I jumped on her face just before sunrise and she screamed with glee. An objectively great start to any special day. To thank me, we went to Utica P-A-R-K! I haven't peed there in so long. It's cool and crisp up here right now in the Catoctin Mountains, and I love it. The only problem is Mommy makes us stop for stoopid pictures every ten feet. #ShesSoAnnoying I refuse to smile or look at the camera because I don't want to reinforce her bad behavior. But she persists. Enjoy these pictures of me scowling. #ImStillHandsomeTho

My books are selling out in the local stores faster than we can resupply. Mommy says that's a good sign. The second book comes out in just a few weeks, and I can't wait!! Mommy has been very busy working on my empire lately. Now she's making pins and boards on Pinterest for me. #ShesAnExcellentMinion

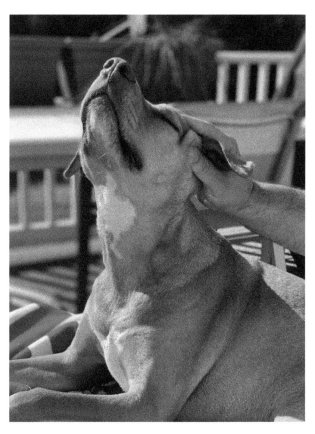

I'm very happy to report the Frederick County Public Libraries in Maryland have decided to carry my book!!! I want to go halp with reading time. The audience would be delicious. I've found that the little hoomans can't squirm away as fast as adults.
#AndTheyreUsuallySticky

Mommy says I'm going to see Scott and my friends at K9 Camp on Monday!!! Mommy's birthday week is working out pretty good for me so far!! #ICantWait #IHopeScottRemembersMe

That's all the news and #Finnanigans from this week. Over and out.

Week One Hundred Thirty-Two

September 19, 2020 ·

HI EVERYONE. FINN HERE with my week 132 report. It was a wild and crazy week!! I got to go see Scott and my friends at K9 Camp on Monday!!!!! It was so much fun. There were 21 dogs that day, and 12 were under a year old. They were extra fun and wore me out fast. But I was still able to get in my licks. #TheKissyBanditStrikesAgain #ImStillTired

On Tuesday I got to visit my allergist, Dr. Jeffers! He's so nice and lets me give him lots of kisses. He said I'm delightful and gave the hoomans medicine for my ears and rears. He thinks my itchies aren't from food, so maybe I can get back some yumyums if this new medicine halps!!

#GimmeBackMyYogurt I don't know how he outwits me, but he also won our Q-Tip rematch. #Sorcery

It's officially cozy sweatshirt weather now, so I made Mommy get out my autumn wardrobe. #CozyIsMyColor

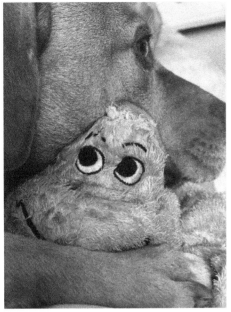

We have been experiencing some unfortunate backsliding on the nigh nigh front lately. The Squishy One is getting fussy about the cold weather protocols. As per standard procedure, around dead-of-night o'clock, I stand up and put my front paws on the side of the bed then smack her with one or both paws until she wakes. #KnockKnock She is then required to raise up the blankets up exactly 29.4567 inches for me to gain entry. I curl up into a croissant between her legs so she can't move (for her own safety), and I'm surrounded by the heat radiators. What's so hard about this? She's been all, "No, Finnnnnn!" and "Staaaaaahpppit, I need some sleep, Finn!"

#ThisMadnessWillNotStand #ICanVomitAnytimeIWant

Mommy says my second book comes out very soon!!! To celebrate, we made vinyl glass clingy things of my gorgeous face. Last night during our walk, we Finn-bombed some of our friends' front doors and car windows. Who doesn't need more of my face in their life? #FinningIsWinning

She's preparing the big table for operation pawtographs, packing and postage, round two. She says the books should be here by mid-October, and I need to get ready to do my part. I keep explaining I have people for that. #ShesThePeople

That's all the news and #Finnanigans from this week. Over and out.

Special Report

Happy Monday, everyone. I woke up Mommy and Daddy bright and early with a sunrise vomit in their bed. Some grass and sticks from yesterday's fun.

#IToldYouICouldVomitAnytimeIWanted

"The best part of waking up... is vomit from your pup." Sing that in your head a couple times, then crave some coffee.

Week One Hundred Thirty-Three

September 26, 2020 ·

HI EVERYONE. FINN HERE with my week 133 report. The hoomans have been fairly well behaved this week. On Sunday they took me to a play date with two fun Vizzies named Baxter and Cayenne. Mommy said I wasn't showing my best behavior when I ran straight into their yard and ate a flower from their flower bed. Or when I jumped up on her lap pretending to be tired then strolled across the patio table in search of the open treat bag. Orrrrr when I ambushed the college hooman named Madison by springing into her lap uninvited and aggressively licking her face. I don't see what the problem is. #ImDelightful

Baxter and I ran around their awesome yard and played hard for a long time. Of course, every time the hoomans called me I pretended I didn't hear them. Clearly Baxter and Cayenne missed some classes at the academy. Because they came running every time their hoomans called out. #Neverrrrrr #WhatsThatSquishyCantHearYou

I decided on Tuesday morning it was time to follow through with my threat to retaliate their selfish sleeping arrangements. I proved that I can indeed vomit anytime and anywhere I want. It was so fun to watch them jump up like pumas when I started barfing in their bed. #SunriseVomitSurprise

Mommy has been feeling blue lately and cries sometimes. She says she is OK, just overwhelmed with all the bad news going on around us and missing her job. We've started getting into fights about this. She tries to push me

away when I come to lick her tears. I'm very strong, and she can't fend me off. I always win and she has to let me lick her eyeballs while she laughs and squeals. #MnnnnSalty #IHalp #HoldStillLetMeLoveYou #AllBetterNow

Daddy and I came upon a pretty sky flower on our walk one morning. He has been mounting an annoying camera on my back during walks lately and it caught our discovery. The sky flower was very delicate and also scary. I investigated for some time with sniffs and pounces before barking once and running away. #ISavedDaddyAgain

We've also had some good staff meetings this week. Very productive discussions about my allergies, dinner time, and how annoying Mommy is. Daddy and I were having some quality alone time when Mommy kept trying to cut in. I shot her my best stank eye to back off.
#SideEyeWorldChampion

That's all the news and #Finnanigans from this week. Over and out.

Week One Hundred Thirty-Four

October 3, 2020 ·

HI EVERYONE. FINN HERE with my week 134 report. This week has been full of power struggles. Mostly the hoomans struggling to accept I have all the power. #OhHowTheyTestMe

I ate a dead dragonfly and I must say... a bit too salty. While it wasn't my favorite snack, it was fun watching Mommy freak out and try to save it. She's a riot. She pried my mouf open and stole it. I swear she considered doing mouf-to-mouf. Hello, it was already dead before I cronched, woman. #ShesNotTheSqueakiestToyInTheBin

I went to daycare at Heavenly Hound Hotel on Monday and got a great mani/pedi from Kristin. She does the best work and snuggles me on the floor while she does it!! I get to kiss her face while she works on my nails, and she laughs and laughs. #ShesDelicious

When I got home from daycare, Mommy tried to put musher's wax on my feets. I do not cooperate with this, ever. We generally wrestle and struggle against each other until she gives up. She tried to exploit how tired I was from daycare. We wrestled, I got as much wax on her shirt as possible, I savored my victory, and then fell asleep. #NeverSurrender #NoYOUHoldStillWoman

My second book came out this week. It hit #2 on the Hot New Release list on Amazon and placed on several best seller lists!! This was very exciting, and Mommy was very happy with our good luck. I asked her for the specific conversion formula I could expect for best seller-to-bacon treats for me, but she was evasive. #ShesSoShady A nice lady named Nikki from Australia was the first to read it! Mommy said it was because something boring about time zones. Again, I wasn't listening. #IWasThinkingAboutKissingAKangaroo

On Thursday night, she dragged me onto an author's live cast with two other hoomans. I showed my disdain for being bothered with this. First off, it was after-dark time so I was tired. Second, she was totally hogging my spotlight with all the hooman words and claiming SHE was the author! I wasn't having it. So I only marginally cooperated by shooting some dirty looks into the camera and knocking into it every so often. Comments from viewers were all about how cute I am and nothing at all about her. #ServesHerRight #GetOutOfMySpotlightWoman

Karen (the purple rubber chicken for those of you just joining us) and I got into a kerfuffle during Friday's afternoon team huddle. It was Friday and everyone was feeling punchy for the weekend, I guess. We went through our afternoon call schedules and what tasks we had left to complete for the work week. Then Daddy asked what we should have for dinner, and I said roasted chicken, bacon and frozen dairy slop, as I always do. Karen flew into a rage and squawked something about marigolds and sunflower seeds. She said we shouldn't eat chickens, and Mommy tried to explain we don't eat rubber chickens, just the other kind. That seemed to calm her down a little. Mommy got some nice pictures of us when we made up. #CalmDownKaren #ShesSoDramatic

Daddy and I have also been practicing with the GoPro so you can see more of life from my view. This week's video shows two things that happened during one of our walks. First, I refused to walk the direction Daddy wanted and we had a sit-off. It's like a stand-off, but we do it sitting down. Daddy got mad when I decided we should go a different way. He made me sit because he thought I would forget which way I wanted to go. Then he plopped down on the sidewalk next to me and lectured me about being willful or something. I don't really know what he said. I wasn't listening. I hope the neighbors didn't see this display of stupid. I hate when we have a battle of wills. #EspeciallyWhenHeWins #WhichImNotSayingIsWhatHappened

Then, he got in a huff and said, "Fine. We're going home." This led to the slug-off. I decided to show him who's in charge by pouncing on and eating a slug as we approached the front door. He got mad and stole it out of my mouf. It's so adorable when he tries to get bossy and yell, "No." He even wagged his finger at me. Oh no, not the finger wag. I'm sooo scared. #Not The camera almost captures my eye roll, if you look closely.
#HowAboutThoseDadShoes #AndSocks

#NineteenEightySixCalledAndTheyWantTheirShoesBack #Burn #NowWhoWon

Also, check out my new list of favorite things on my website!

That's all the news and #Finnanigans from this week. Over and out.

Week One Hundred Thirty-Five

October 10, 2020 ·

HI EVERYONE. FINN HERE with my week 135 report. After all the fun last week with the sunrise vomit surprise, I thought I should shake things up again. This time I gifted the hoomans on Sunday with a pre-sunrise bootyjuice bomb in their bed. They loved it. You should have heard all the, "Oh Fiiinnnnn!" and, "Whyyyyyyy?!" They jumped up to pull away the sheets before the booty juice could seep down to the feather bed, and they got everything into the washing machine in mere minutes. The Squishy One seemed impressed that I managed to stickify and stinkify both the bottom and top sheets in one foul explosion. #ExtraCreditForDistance

I was in the newspaper again, too! What can I say, celebrity suits me. People can't get enough of my dapper good looks and charm. This time the Cape Gazette!! I think this objectively qualifies me for greater respect and an improved treat schedule at home.

We got to see some of my favorite littles in the neighborhood this week. They belong to a pretty dog named Andie. She pretends not to like me, but we all know that's just a sign she has a crush on me. As we walked past her house, Andie's little hooman, Elliana, excitedly shouted across the way to us that she lost her first tooth and got $5 from the tooth fairy. I asked the Squishy One what this meant, and she explained a Santa-like "fairy" (aka intruder) brings children money in exchange for their chompers. At least Santa doesn't demand body parts when he brings prezzies. #BlackMarketTeethForSale #DoesAnyoneElseFindThisAlarming

Landon, Andie's biggest little, showed us his Finn sticker up in his bedroom window and said he can't wait to read book two!! #IThinkHeLovesMe Then

Andie's littlest little hooman, Grayson, showed us his new rope! It looked very tuggable, but my hoomans wouldn't let me go over and play tug of war with him. #ILoveLittles

I WANT YOU TO THROW IT, BUT I DONT WANT TO GIVE IT TO YOU.
— FINNEGAN COUNT SMOOSHIE TUSHIE

The other big news of the week is the progress I'm making with Operation Woo Stella. The Squishy One found out from Stella's Mommy that Stella is going to start attending a new play place up in Rehoboth called "Doggies at the Beach." So I convinced my Mommy to get me in up there! I had my "attitude check" interview on Friday and passed with flying colors. Everyone loved me and I established myself quickly as Rehoboth's newest kissy bandit. Now all I have to do is make sure I go play the same day that Stella is there, and my plan will be set in motion! I'll play hard to get until she falls for me. #FancyMeetingYouHere #ComeHereOften #OfAllTheGinJoints #Stelluhhhhhh

It was also a good week for prezzies. I found a dead snake skin that Mommy wouldn't let me keep and a dead frog that Daddy wouldn't let me keep. Prezzies I did get to keep included a handsome new bandana with my name on it, and I even got some new amazing Avengers jammies! #HulkSmash

Mommy says I have to sign off now because we have 120 books to pawtograph, package and ship!! #MyWorkIsNeverDone

That's all the news and #Finnanigans from this week. Over and out.

Week One Hundred Thirty-Six

October 17, 2020 ·

HI EVERYONE. FINN HERE with my week 136 report. I scored a second date with Stella at her house on Sunday!! I think she likes me!! We rubbed noses and played as best we could with our dumb chaperones hovering. Isn't she the dreamiest? #SecondDateMoves #Stelluhhhhh

After my date with Stella, I was in the mood for adventure. So the hoomans and I drove out to a big sunflower field. I envisioned running through the field with the wind in my ears and maybe sampling some of the cuisine. But they wouldn't let me do any of that! "Don't eat the bee, Finn!" and "No! You can't eat the sunflower, Finn!" You can see in the evidence photos that I was salty the whole time. I refused to smile or participate in their dumb pictures. #SaltyGlareWorldChampion #IWannaEatTheBee

The boxes of book two arrived this week, and I got Mommy in gear right away on processing everyone's orders. She says I'm supposed to halp her more with the pawtographing, and I say I have people for that. We pawtographed and shipped 130 books in four days this week!! Everyone should be getting them in their mailboxes soon and we're excited to see the new #ImWithFinn posts and to see where everyone puts their surprise Finn window cling prezzie! #OhBabyThePlacesIllGo #LemmeSeeMeOnYourWindows

Dr. Jeffers gave me some new oral steroids that have halped my ears so

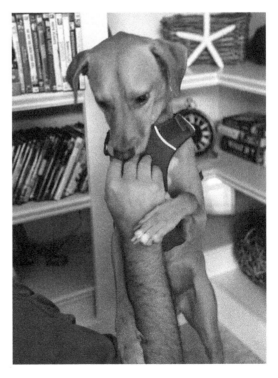

much. And that means no more horrible-no-good-evil allergy drops in my ears anymore!! Although, I will miss our wrastling matches and hearing Mommy screech when more got on her than in my ears. I'm not shaking my head and miserable anymore. So Mommy says we might go for a hike today!! #ILoveHikes #ILoveDrJeffers

I made even more progress on Operation Woo Stella during the week. I leveraged my exceptional leadership skills to orchestrate our hoomans into taking us to the new play place on the same day. I strolled into Doggies at the Beach like I owned the place. I ran over and gave Stella kisses then switched to "hard-to-kiss" mode. She mostly ignored me, having no patience for my nonsense. But she didn't pay anyone else any attention either. So, I'll take it! #IWantYouToWantMe #DontHateThePlayerHateTheGame

I made another newspaper today, too! The Frederick News Post did an article about me and my books!! It's a little too much about the transcriber and not enough about the brains and style of the operation, if you ask me. But they spelled her last name wrong so there's some justice in that. #QuitHoggingTheSpotlightRomak

The hoomans tried to take pictures of me with my second masterpiece today. I think the outtakes are better than the serious ones. #ButImDashingInAllOfThem

That's all the news and #Finnanigans from this week. Over and out.

Special Report
October 22, 2020 ·

I have prepared the following agenda for my playdate with Stella at our house today:

1. Tandem walk to hunt for hoppies, jumpies, and escargot and to pee on stuff.

2. Cuddle in my extra-large dog bed while Mommy prepares us a snack.

3. Snack.

4. Show Stella all the fun toys I have for chewing on.

5. Chew on toys.

6. Recreate the scene from Lady and the Tramp. (Mommy says it's too soon for this but she's stoopid.)

7. More walkies.

8. Naps.

9. Chase me, tug of war, or "No, it's mine!" for at least an hour.

10. Zoomies.

I'm now waiting patiently in my bow tie by the front door for her arrival.
#Stelluhhhhhh #ThirdDate

Week One Hundred Thirty-Seven

October 24, 2020 ·

HI EVERYONE. FINN HERE with my week 137 report. It's been a STELLAr week! More on that in a moment. There's a lot of pics this week because it was just that great of a week. And lots of videos on FinnTube, too. #GoWatchThemHoomans

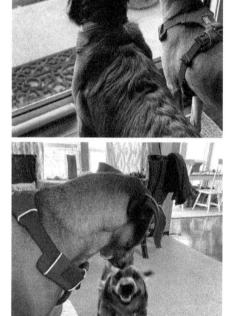

On Saturday, I took the hoomans to the boardwalk to check in on Tony and see if he had any bacon. He didn't answer my totally-appropriate and objectively reasonable screams from outside his door this time though. Mommy said he was busy with a long line of customers. I think he should've dropped everything to scratch my bacon itch. #AndUnderMyChin #DoesntHeKnowWhoIAm

After that disappointment, Daddy and I ran and played on the sand a while. We chased some beach chickens and even ran after some kind of string-bird. It bounced around in the sky, zig zagging in the wind. Daddy called it a kite. I called it dangerous! I was never able to reach it, but it crashed to the ground anyway, cowered by fear of me and my scary barking, I guess. #ItKnowsWhosBoss #SubmitStringBirdSubmit

Unfortunately, we also ran into a terrifying sand creature the hoomans called a horseshoe crab. I called it danger seafood. I tried to tell them to be careful, but they had no fear of it. It was dark brown and mysterious. A hard shell and pointy butt. How could that not be dangerous!?! #YouCantFixStupid #ButYouCanSaveThem

During the week, we did two evening hikes that ended in the bayside sand! They were awesome. One night, we hit a small area where the sunset is especially beautiful. I had to save us again, this time from a sketchy-looking danger log. Mommy said it was "just" a piece of driftwood with mussels growing on it. I told her she's "just" a fool and to back away from it. I barked a good long while, ruining the peaceful sunset for all the other folks nearby. Eventually, the danger log got the message and drifted away so we could enjoy the pretty colors in the sky.
#ThisIsTheLife

Paws down, the highlight of the week was my playdate with Stella at my house!! I put on my fancy bow tie and planned a great day for us. She came over in a pretty pink number, and we had a blast. Mommy was so annoying and wouldn't leave us alone. Just like she does with me and Daddy time. #JealousMuch #BackOffThirdWheel

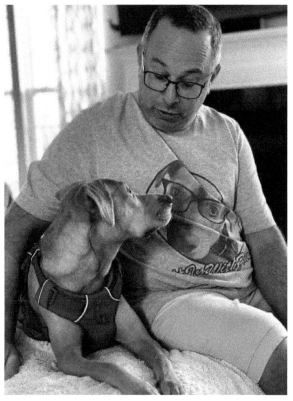

#Stelluhhhhhh

I showed Stella my toys and let her chew on each one for almost ten seconds before taking them back. #ImGenerousThatWay We made several couple-walks through the neighborhood so I could show her off and make clear to the others that's she's taken. We sniffed what needed sniffin', peed on what needed peeing on, wrestled, had tandem zoomies and even did tandem neighborhood patrols at the front door. The squirrels didn't even know what hit 'em. She's a dreamboat to be sure. But she has so much energy. After a couple hours, I was ready for a nap and she was still going. I stopped to ask Daddy for girl-advice, and he explained this is the risk of settling down with a younger woman.

That night, we went for another hike. This time to James Farm Park. We again encountered a danger seafood, but this one was much bigger and more threatening. We also met a small dog named Hoot on the bay beach, and we

sniffed all the sniffs. The bay side has such delightful murky sniffs. Seaweed, teeny danger seafoods that run sideways, shells, and rotting fish flesh. It's an olfactory overload of amazing. #SmellThis

Check out the amazing videos from <u>my danger seafood</u> and <u>danger log encounters</u> and some go-pro footage that allows you to take a dog's eye view hike with me at James Farm Park on my FinnTube channel at: https://www.youtube.com/c/FinnTheDog

That's all the news and #Finnanigans from this week. Over and out.

Week One Hundred Thirty-Eight

November 7, 2020 ·

#StartingToThinkTheresAConnection

HI EVERYONE. FINN HERE with my week 138 report. I will never understand these hoomans. Last weekend was the annual ritual they call Howloween. Note that when I howl, they carry on and tell me to shush. But they get to have a whole holiday about it. #Unfair #AndTheyDontEvenHowl

Several weeks ago, the hoomans bought me another orange porch orb. It's mine apparently. I'm just not allowed to play with it or pee on it. I named him Billy and tried not to get attached, because I knew from last year what was going to happen to him. #NothingGood

I sniffed and licked Billy each time we passed him on the porch, and sometimes I pretended like I was gonna pee on him just to get a rise out of the hoomans. I did my best to comfort him and make his last days good ones. He clearly had no idea what was coming. #SometimesThatsBetter

Well, last weekend was the day of reckoning for poor Billy. Mommy, rather unceremoniously, chopped off his head and scooped out the insides of my round orange friend. #RIPBilly His insides smelled just like the delicious orange fluff I get on my dinner every night.

My suspicion deepened when she cooked the innards and whirred them up in her loud choppy machine. They smelled so good. I don't know how, but she turned the stringy goopy intestines of my porch orb friend into my dinner fluff. #IFeltGuiltyButStillAteHim

Then I supervised Daddy stringing bags of candy onto ropes on the front porch. He did this joyfully as if there was some happy reason to take inside foodstuffs and hang them on ropes outside. #Lunatic

Next up in the house of horrors, Mommy dressed me in a devil costume and said it was a reflection of real life, whatever

that means. But everyone who saw me called me a "handsome little devil," so I went with it. She dressed Daddy in a big chicken costume and made us take pictures. #ShesTheWorst #ILikePickingMyOwnOutfits

Small children came and stole the candy bags from our porch, and this seemed to please the freaks. Daddy just stood there waving and yelling "Happy Howloween!" to the little marauders through the glass door!! It was mayhem. Their disguises didn't fool me, though. I recognized all of them!! I did my best to take charge, barking to scare them off. And, please let the record reflect, I was 100% successful.
#YoureWelcomeYouFools

On Sunday, we woke up and pretended like none of it happened. I took the hoomans to the boardwalk to clear my head. Thank Dog, Tony was available for a bacon and kisses consult. He comforted me while I cronched on his delicious bacon and told him about my hard time the night before. He felt so bad for me, I scored another piece of bacon!!!! #DoubleBaconIsEverything #TonyJustGetsMe

Mommy spent most of the week willfully ignoring me while she banged on her pooter and yacked on the phone. #Boring

She said she was setting up a new consulting business that's not about me or even dogs. Something about boring anti-corruption, ethics and compliance stuff. #Snooze But I saw her logo over her shoulder and was horrified to find it not only has a dog on it, but it's NOT ME. I'm livid and preparing a detailed report to HR. She can't produce a signed conflict of interest waiver. #ThisWillNotStand

I barfed again this morning despite a week of chicken and rice and 11 p.m. feedings. #ThatllShowEm #DrRichardsHereICome

That's all the news and #Finnanigans from this week. Over and out.

Week One Hundred Thirty-Nine

November 14, 2020 ·

HI EVERYONE. FINN HERE with my week 139 report. I saw Dr. Richards last week for my tummy troubles. I was more shy than usual and even a little scared, which really isn't like me. My tummy really hurt, and I was nervous. Dr. Richards gave me kisses and reminded me I'm the goodest boy. Then she gave me some medicine to halp my tummy. She told Mommy I'd lost a couple pounds and gave her instructions for halping me calm down my yumyum processing system. #AkaPoopMaker #AkaNoiseMaker

I talked Dr. Richards into telling the hoomans I require home-cooked chicken and rice with pumpkin purée for twice daily bonus meals. And I don't know how, but it worked!!!! Well, sorta. There was some kind of miscommunication because the hoomans think the chicken and rice replace my meals when clearly, they are supposed to be extra meals. I've been protesting twice a day for my usual morning and evening kibble time, to no avail. #ItsMadnessHere #DoggieOCDIsReal

I've noticed some strange things going on this week with my yumyum processing system. Three times this week, my booty has let out squeaky butt-puffs. Each time it has startled me, and I've looked to the Squishy One for assurance that nothing is inside there crying to get out. I'm not usually one for butt-puffery anyway but, usually if it does happen, it's what Grandpa calls, "silent but deadly." A lovely aroma sneaks out, and I linger nearby to

enjoy it. But now the aroma is preceded by a butt-puff squeak! #IGuessTheyAreProtestingToo

I'm also making mouf-puffs. Right after I eat, I climb into the Squishy One's lap and mouf-puff right in her face. She loves it. #TastesLikeChicken She is keeping a detailed log of my eats, poops, mouf-puffs, butt-puffs, and mopeyness for Dr. Richards. #ShesAFreak

There was one really bright spot this week. One of our nice neighbors brought over the DE *Beach Life Magazine* last night and guess what? There was an article all about me!!! It's on shiny paper and everything! How fun! A funny author and local celebrity named Fay Jacobs wrote all about adorable me and included my Viking hat picture. Mommy loves Fay's funny books and says you should check them out. #TheCampingStoryIsHerFavorite

Mommy says we're going to talk to lots of littles next week over the pooter to teach them how they can grow up to be authors and creators, too. She got great ideas and halp from our friends with ways to make the classes fun and interactive for the littles. Three thousand kids.... Whoa! I hope I can smell them through the pooter. #StillInvestigating #LittlesAreMyFavorite

That's all the news and #Finnanigans from this week. Over and out.

Special Report
November 16, 2020 ·

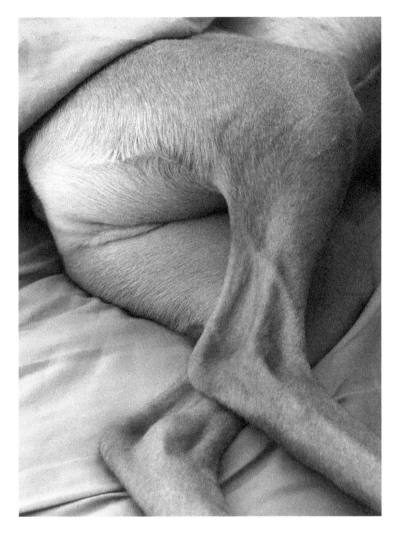

Good morning, Devil Woman. The cannon is loaded. Prepare for butt-puff!!!

Special Report

November 19, 2020 ·

The stages of found old/new toy napping.

Ma! Ma! I found this smelly old dragon toy in the bin in that closet I'm not supposed to go into. It smells like Mr. Snuggles. Maaaaa! Looooook at my dragon.

Can you hold me and my dragon? Just for a minute okay? LOOOOOK AT MY DRAGON!!! But don't touch it.

I'm getting sleepy. Maybe dragon and I should just nap in your arms for a while, okay?

Week One Hundred Forty

November 21, 2020 ·

HI EVERYONE. FINN HERE with my week 140 report. This week has been super fun!!! The Squishy One and I have been talking to littles through the computer about my books and how to be an author like me. The littles are very cute and say funny things. My favorite part is always the wiggle-butt dance break where they wag their tails like me! My only complaint is that I can't smell, taste, or steal anything from the littles because they are trapped inside the computer. #PleaseLetThemOut #LittlesAreUsuallyStickyAndDelicious

After the computer kidnaps them, the littles email me their stories and drawings. The Squishy One halps me with special replies for each little. Last night, we read a story written by a little about her dog named Booger. Booger peed in his crate. #PoorBooger

We also had TWO newspaper stories about me this week. Count 'em... two! The Carteret News Times wrote a wonderful article about me, and how I came into rescue down in Swansboro, NC. Mommy said it's also about how adorable I am. The reporter spoke to the nice lady from the shelter and found out my name was once Cupid. Mommy laughs and laughs every time she hears that. She says that's ironic, and I'm trying to find out what that word means. #SoundsMetallic

The other article was by a nice lady in Delaware for the Sussex Living, Daily Times, and Delmarva Now papers! It's also about how adorable I am.

#OfCourse Mommy says it's also about how much fun we have on social media, thanks to you guys. #FINNaticsAreTheBest

If you want to read those articles and see all my media coverage, check out my web page! I've had Mommy and Daddy adding lots of fun stuff to my website. Mommy also wrote a blog article about why we started writing the books. #GoTakeALook #ThereIsAWholePageOfHeadshots #ImAdorable

My tummy is still rumbly but getting a little better. I heard Mommy on the phone with Dr. Richards describing all my mouf-puffs and butt-puffs in great detail. I'm still getting my gourmet chicken and rice with a side of pumpkin purée, but no kibble. I'm used to it now, so I've stopped the protest concerts. Mommy says I'll probably scream about the chicken and rice going away when we do switch back to kibble. #ShesNotWrong #IDontLikeChange

I've had a lot of Canadian air chicken traffic control duties this week. Entire squawkdrons of threatening Canadian air chickens fly in a V-shaped formation through my air space and clearly require navigational support. I bark to point them south, and they obey my command. I like when my authority is respected. #ISavedUsAllAgain #NotOnMyWatch #IAmABirdDogAfterAll

I found an old dragon stuffie in that bin I'm not supposed to go into that's inside that closet I'm not supposed to go into. He smells so good. I ran to show Mommy my treasure, and she said he belonged to Mr. Snuggles. She cried a little because she misses him, but decided to let me keep his dragon. Dragon and I have gone on two walkies, napped on Mommy's lap, and he's even been caught spooning Karen while Corporal Ducky watches. #ItsJustCuddling #DontMakeItWeird

Mommy says we're going to have Thanksgiving yumyums next week and that means these nutcases will soon put up that imposter tree with all the shiny spinny danglies I'm not supposed to play with. But it also means turkey, and I love turkey. #MaybeSomeMoreHomemadePumpkinPuree

That's all the news and #Finnanigans from this week. Over and out.

Week One Hundred Forty One

November 28, 2020 ·

HI EVERYONE. FINN HERE with my week 141 report. Ugh. The imposter tree is back. This may be the year I can no longer resist testing their resolve on this charade. #TreesAreForPeeingOn

The Squishy One is torturing Daddy and me with endless Christmas music. I'm starting to crack already. And based on his muttering and crazy eyes, so is Daddy. #MakeItStop #MeleKalikimakaIsTheWorst

To celebrate Thanksgiving, I signed us up for an Author Takeover Day on Friday, where we had to post every hour into a Facebook book club group to halp people get to know us. But I lost interest after an hour and made Mommy do it. She calls it slacking, I call it effective outsourcing/low-cost labor management. You'll be relieved to know everyone in the group agreed I'm delightful and adorable. #ClearlyWiseHoomans

The highlight of the week was our Viz Whizz meet up this morning at Marci's house. We got to see Betsi and Auggie, and also Baxter and Cayenne again. And we made new friends: Bourbon, Scout and Willow. Willow was a zippy and confident 4-month-old cutie that took no guff from anyone. She hung with the big dogs like a queen. I'd like her to be my queen. #HubbaHubba #StellaIsOutWillowIsIn #SorryStella #NotReally

Scout was roughly the size of a horse and his brother Baxter and I engaged in an epic hump-battle to win Willow's affection and establish dominance in the pack. When Baxter, 30-lbs. larger, started humping me, I heard Mommy laughing and saying, "Serves him right!" and "That's how you make Jamieson feel at daycare, Finn." #ShesTheWorst #IThinkIWonThough

There is a great big bafftub on the property with a dock. We were all innocently playing when I heard all the hoomans yell, "Ffffffiiiiiinnnnn!" in near-unison. I looked up, confused, then realized they were celebrating my amazing mud find. I was shoulder deep in the delightful mud-frosting, snorkeling for sticks, and they couldn't have been more thrilled. I ran up to each one and jumped up on them to be part of the celebration. Each one squealed with glee as I coated them in the mud frosting, too. #YoureWelcome #ThatsBetter

I really liked seeing Betsi and Auggie again. I sidled up to Betsi a few times for lovin's, and she did not disappoint. #WeLoveBetsi

Best of all, Marci gifted us two huge pumpkins from her porch, so Mommy is making me more homemade purée as I paw. #ShesAGoodWorker #EvenThoughShesLippy

I also took the hoomans for a quick romp on the beach, because Becca told Mommy we had to go outside and enjoy the nice day. #ThanksBecca We

turbo-dug for the sideways-walkers, chased beach chickens, and splashed in the water. We also saw the biggest, noisiest, yellowest beach chicken up in the air. It was menacing, but I scared it off. #ISavedEveryone

Mommy wrote an article for a magazine in a far-away land called California. It's about me, my adorableness, and the story of how I came to rescue these hoomans in more ways than one.

That's all the news and #Finnanigans from this week. Over and out.

Week One Hundred Forty-Two
December 5, 2020 ·

HI EVERYONE. FINN HERE with my week 142 report. The situation with the imposter tree has taken an ugly turn. No, I didn't pee on it. #Yet But, some of the blinky flashy things aren't working, so the hoomans haven't yet put on the sparkly dangly things. Daddy sits with it every night and fights with it. He and the imposter tree wrestle some, and then Daddy says mean things to it. I think imposter tree is in trouble. #ServesHimRight #ImWinning

Mommy's mass production of pumpkin mush continued all week. She is asking friends and neighbors for their porch orbs and turning them into my beloved pumpkin mush!! So far, she's made about ten gallons to freeze. #ShesDelightedWithHerself I'm exhausted from all the supervising and crying to initiate proper taste-test protocols. #WhyDoesntSheFollowProtocols

I was super excited Thursday morning when Mommy told me Jess was coming over for a date. I waited by the door with my two favorite toys to greet her. But when she came, she betrayed me. She cut my nails!! #TheHorror #DremelsAreToolsOfTheDevil

On Friday, Mommy and I talked to more littles trapped in the computer. These were the littlest littles so far. Mommy called them first-graders. They giggled at my videos, and when I sniffed the screen. I don't understand why I can't smell or taste them. #TheyLookDelicious I especially enjoyed the wiggle-butt dance break when

Mommy asked them to get up and wag their tails like a dog.
#ButTheyDidntDoItRight
#TheirTailsAreTooShort

It's very cold here now, and I don't like it. Even with my turtleneck, I'm freezing during our walks. As soon as we're home, I run and jump on Mommy for halp. Sometimes she's asleep and screams when my cold wet paws make landing on her face. #CryBaby

A review of my first book made it into *Publisher's Weekly Magazine,* and Mommy is very excited that a man named Keanu Reeves is on the cover. She says that practically makes them best friends now and she's waiting for his call. #DontDoItKeanu #ShesClingy

That's all the news and #Finnanigans from this week. Over and out.

Special Report
December 8, 2020 ·

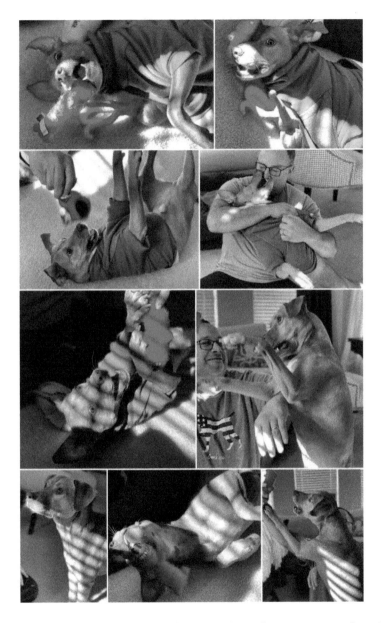

We held a mid-day team huddle to discuss the afternoon work schedule. But things got out of hand when Smiley the Sausage got lippy with me about someone abusing the free cookies in the break room.

Week One Hundred Forty-Three

December 12, 2020 ·

HI EVERYONE. FINN HERE with my week 143 report. The holidays are now in full swing here at the crib. Daddy won the battle of lights with the imposter tree, and it's now adorned with danglies and sparklies galore. #HowItTauntsMe

We are also celebrating Hanukkah again. I'm mesmerized by the candles each year and how Daddy talks funny as he lights them. We sit in the living room and watch them burn down and talk about what we wish for in the New Year. #MostlyTreats

One evening, Mommy said we should take a Christmakkuh picture in front of the tree. I acquiesced, knowing it would at least mean treats and a few minutes of really frustrating her. #ILiveForThat

Usually this involves a few, "Finn. Finn. Watch me. Finnnn!" or silly noises to make me look up. I always ignore my name, but she can't halp trying. The noises used to work but I'm onto her now. She usually gets me with the tried and true, "Doooo youuuuuu wannnnna?" business. Of course, I wanna. I wanna on a cellular level, so usually my eyes and ears betray me with an adorable, head-tilted look at the camera. #ICantFightMyCutenessForLong

But not this time. This time they betrayed me with the most horrendous of embarrassing props! This time they got stoopid glasses involved. You can see from the evidence attached that I did not capitulate. Even the old, "Do you wanna?" ruse didn't

work. Would I make an adorable reindeer? Of course! Do I want glasses touching and hiding my gorgeous face? #NEVER #EvenIHaveMyLimits #RetaliationIsForthcoming

We also fought that evening about my llama pajamas. It wasn't really about the pajamas so much as Mommy being a jerk. As is protocol, she presented me with two PJ options for the evening, and I nosed the Christmas Llamas. They're adorable. I'm adorable. It's a perfect match. #AndLlamaPajamaRhymes

While she was getting me suited up, I got distracted by something Daddy was crinkling in the kitchen and took off to investigate. #ItCouldveBeenFood #IHadNoChoice

This resulted in my business-end left un-pajama'd and nakey. I went to my place and put on a pretty great pop-up concert protest to convey my irritation at her sloppy work. Then she has the nerve to say, "Come here Finn and I'll fix it." Come to her? #AbsolutelyNot

She's gotten way too big for her britches lately and needed a reminder who's boss around here. I screamed back at her that she needed to come to me. I was the victim in this mess. It was my bum that was exposed to the cold night air! This "discussion" went on for some time until we both hunkered down, silently

resolved, in our own corners. #AtLeastSheWasSilentForAChange

Our standoff lasted until the next morning when I forgot about our fight and accidentally ran to Mommy for our usual PJ-removal process. She gleefully removed the front end of my jammies and asked if it was worth my bum being cold all night. #ItWas

The freaks have also installed an imposter fireplace in the bedroom noise-box. Where there are usually hoomans trapped inside endlessly yapping, it's now fake fire. It looks and sounds like fire, but it doesn't make heat or smells. We cuddle together in bed and watch the fake fire make fake fire noises, and the hoomans seem soothed. They're so enamored with imposter things. #WhateverWorks #YouFreaks

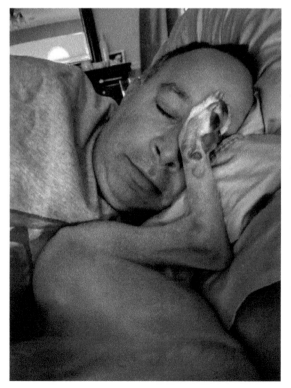

We talked to more littles trapped inside the screen on Wednesday. These littles were from a faraway land called Oregon. They called themselves "prairie dogs" but looked nothing like dogs at all. #StillInvestigating #AndIDontKnowWhatAPrairieIs They were delightful littles and made my Mommy giggle a lot. They showed us their pets and told us about their weekly writing workshop. But don't worry, I was still the cutest of all the pets. #AGoodTimeWasHadByAll #WeLoveLittles

Speaking of writing workshops, I've really been cracking down on

Mommy this week, and we've made serious progress on my new book. If she can stay focused and work half as hard as I do, we might have it ready to publish in February. #ValentinesDaySmiles

That's all the news and #Finnanigans from this week. Over and out.

Week One Hundred Forty-Four

December 19, 2020 ·

HI EVERYONE. FINN HERE with my week 144 report. I got a surprise visit from Stella last weekend. I was so excited that you can see my paw quivering as I try to unlock the door for her (in this video). As a direct result of my idiot hoomans trying to put those awful Christmas glasses on her for a picture, SHE BROKE UP WITH ME. She said she just wants to be frens and something about my playboy ways, constantly cheating on her, having no manners and being too kissy. Those are all suspiciously vague, so I think we can all agree that was all just a cover for the glasses. #Stelluhhhhhh #ThanksALotDevilWoman

I caught The Squishy One feeding a huge reindeer! He was laying in our yard, and she was feeding him apple slices. I tried to warn her to stop, but she wouldn't listen. She kept saying, "It's just a deer," and I kept saying, "You don't know what 'just' means!" He was really, really tall and had spikes coming out of his head. SPIKES!! Yeah, devil woman, those spikes are there for cuddling, I'm sure. #YouFool Then I overheard her tell Daddy she named him Bucky, and we're keeping him. Thankfully, Daddy talked her out of bringing him in the house. #ShesTheWorst

We had a surprise warm day this week, so I took the hoomans to the beach. It was empty, so we got to play for a long time. I chased all the beach chickens and dug for sidewalkers! Daddy and I ran up and down the water line, daring it to touch us. #ChaseMe #ButDontCatchMe

A gigantic sky dinosaur they call "a heron" has made a nest in the creek next to our house. It's the biggest and scariest sky monster I've ever seen. Mommy said they are very strong and can even eat baby alligators, so I shouldn't antagonize it. But I can't halp myself. #ItsNotGonnaBarkAtItself #WhatsAnAlligator

Every morning at o-dark-thirty, I carry on and bark to alert the whole neighborhood to the danger. I tug and pull on my leash like I would attack it if only I could break free from those bonds. Daddy tells me to hush and drags me until I start walking again. It's our new morning routine, and everyone loves it. #ExceptTheHeron

In other wildlife news, Foxy Roxy is also back. I've known she was back for some time, but the hoomans never listen to me when I alert to her scent. Daddy finally saw her on the doorbell camera and now, all of a sudden, she's real. I have the most sophisticated sniffer device in the world, and yet they ignore me. #WhenWillTheyLearn

It's gotten cold and rainy here. I do not like. I miss the white fluffy stuff we had at the primary dwelling. I wonder if I scared it away by murdering all those snowmen and women. #ImSorryFrosty #ComeBack

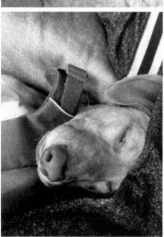

In wonderful news, I found where the hoomans hid my petrified cheese bar and managed to steal it back!! We've had a wonderful week of shiv making. I bring it to them and drop on either their hand or face and say #HoldDis. They usually do, and I work to whittle it into the shape of a weapon. They get so whiney about having to hold it for me. #CantFindGoodHalpAnymore

The Squishy One got especially fussy one night and put it on the side table. She told me to leave it, and I told her to shut it. Words ensued and things escalated. I told her I can jump up and get it whenever I want, and she said, "Oh, yeah?" #ThatsNeverGood

Moments later, I found my beloved petrified cheese bar trapped underneath the horrible, no good, awful Christmas glasses. She'd outsmarted me, knowing I wouldn't risk contact with those things again. #IllGetYouForThisDevilWoman #ICanVomitAnytimeIWant

I've finally gotten the Hairy One to cooperate with shiv making, and it's really bonding us more. I dominate him while he holds it for me. I paw his hands the way I want it held. And we make lots of eye contact while he covets my precious. #AllIsRightInTheWorld

That's all the news and #Finnanigans from this week. Over and out

Special Report

December 21, 2020 ·

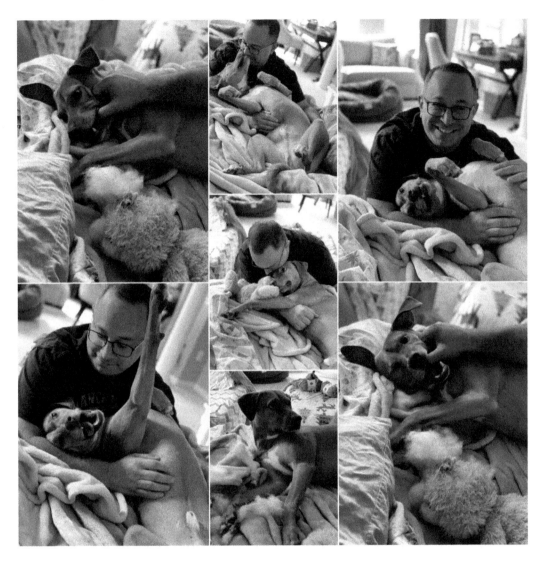

Bunny joined our staff meeting this afternoon and things got ruff. She muttered something about me always being late on my project deliverables, and I took offense.

Then, without any kind of trial or verdict, I disemboweled her for her crimes. #SheWasntWrongThough #RIPBunny

Special Report

December 23, 2020 ·

Santa Paws stopped by for Festivus!!! I performed feats of strength and aired many, many grievances. #SoMany

Week One Hundred Forty-Five
December 26, 2020 ·

HI EVERYONE. FINN HERE with my week 145 report. Well, it happened again. Despite my best efforts, somehow Santa Paws got past me, again! I did extra neighborhood patrols all evening on the smellout for those reindeer and sniffed nothing. I don't know how he does it! #Sorcery

But it's not all bad because he left me prezzies!!! My first prezzie was the tissue paper that covered my other prezzies. I just love tissue paper. #TissuePaperCausesZoomies

My other prezzies included a colossal crab stuffie named Biff and a new ducky named Fleet Admiral Fiona Flapper. Only trouble is she thinks she's the boss of us. She says Fleet Admiral outranks Captain and Corporal. #WeAreDubious Cap'n Ducky and Corporal Ducky are resisting her authority and I'm biting her face. #WhosTheBossNowFiona

I also found a new yak cheese bar in my stocking!!!! I love those things! Mommy turned the end of my last one into a big cheese poof, and I loved that too! As you can see in one of the videos, I did have a brief meltdown when no one would hold my cheese bar for me. #CantGetGoodHalpAnymore

Daddy captured my exceptional bravery on video when we were attacked by Canadian air chickens. We were taking fire from everywhere. Canadian air-chicken squawkdrons to the left, to the right, everywhere I spun. It's was mayhem. Mayhem!

The day before the Santa B&E, I took the hoomans to the beach to chase some beach chickens and wish Tony the bacon dealer a merry merry. The whole outing was a disaster. First, we found a huge metal pipe laying in the sand and extending all the way out into the gigantic bafftub. Mommy said it was some kind of beach replenishment operation. My preference for consistency snuck out in the form of a five-alarm meltdown. But my over-the-top howling, barking, and charging at this foreign object didn't seem to halp. #Surprising #UsuallyDoesTheTrick

Then a gaggle of hoomans assembled nearby on the sand. I waited patiently for them to notice me and come running over to adore me. They didn't. So I forced Daddy and me closer and into their line of sight. Nothing. I decided maybe they needed some movement to catch their eyes. Maybe they couldn't see my adorable elf get-up. So I stood up on my back legs and twirled while crying out to them. I spun and hopped and screamed. NOTHING. These hoomans just ignored me. No one came to adore me. No one came to tell me I am the cutest. No "Awwwwwws." No "What a sweeeeet dogggg." Nothing. #Monsters

The Hairy One made a special compilation video montage of all the Christmas Eve and Christmas Day fun for you. But I must warn you, when you get to this next part of the story in the video, it could break you. #ItAlmostBrokeMe

In an effort to soothe my sorrow, Mommy suggests we go see Tony the bacon dealer up on the boardwalk. #GreatIdea #ForAChange He's 100% sure to love on me and tell me I'm adorable. #AndAlsoBacon

So we walked along the boards where even more hoomans ignored me. I heard a few say, "He's cute," and "Love the elf costume," but that was it. No kissies, no lovin's, noooo scratchies. #TheHorror

Of course, Mommy made us stop for stoopid pictures in front of the big Bethany tree, and I generally refused to cooperate. #IWasInAMoodAtThisPoint #NoCutePicsForYouDevilWoman

We made our way to Turtle Beach Cafe only to find my beloved Tony... NOT THERE!!!!! #WhatTheElf I've never seen those doors closed, ever! I pawed at the doors and cried out for my Tony. But no one appeared. #ItWasHeartbreaking #ImSorryYouAllHaveToSeeThis

Mommy tried to tell me some sign in the door said they were on a much-deserved Christmas break for a couple days. She droned on a while about how they work almost every day and rarely get a break. #WhatDoesThisHaveToDoWithMe #WheresTony #DoWeHaveHisHomeAddress

Knowing she's dumb and usually wrong, I ignored her and kept screaming for Tony. Was it the elf get-up? Had Mommy alienated them somehow? Bad things are usually her fault. This was just a disaster. #WhatDidYouDoDevilWoman

Eventually, Daddy pulled me away and told me we could come back after Christmas to see Tony. I looked over my shoulder back at those doors for as long as I could keep them in view. #Toonnnnnnny

The only bright spot from this week other than the prezzies for me is this prezzie for your doggos: my new book is now available!!!!!! This book is a little different from the others. It's loaded with my best advice for doggos everywhere who are trying to manage their hoomans.

"Do you feel like your hoomans aren't giving you the five-star service you deserve? This guide is for all the doggos out there training hoomans to become better servants. Improve your standard of living today! Pawket sized for doggos on the go and in the field. Chock-full of practical tips and proven strategies for getting your hooman to do what you want when you want it! This handy guide covers things like getting off on the right paw with your new hooman, a hooman user's guide, appropriate training strategies, retaliation techniques, and more! You deserve only the best. So make it happen today!"

That's all the news and #Finnanigans from this week. Over and out.

Week One Hundred Forty-Six

January 2, 2021 ·

HI EVERYONE. FINN HERE with my week 146 report. What a week! The weather perked up, so we got lots of extra-long walkies at the boardwalk! In one walk we encountered an over-eager puppy poodle that annoyed me. If you look closely, you can see me asking Daddy, "She's back there, isn't she?" #DaddyHoldMe

Colossal Crab sure is making himself at home around here, and he's mouthy. At one of our morning staff meetings this week he got real uppity. He's brand new to the company, and he's already getting bossy. "How seriously do we take project deadlines? Doesn't seem very serious." "Why is the snack area in the break room ransacked?" "Who's in charge of assigning tasks?" Bunny tried to warn him what happens to snitches, but he didn't listen. #FeedbackIsNotEncouragedHere

But since I'm practicing my new conflict resolution and leadership techniques, I just banished him to the mailroom instead of ripping his face off. #ThatsHowIGetPromoted #SortSomeMailCrabMan #Quietly

Daddy and I have also been enjoying lots of dental diving fun on our walks. I hoover up something I shouldn't, he yells "Finn, no!" Then I try to swallow it as fast as I can while he shoves his meaty paw in my mouf. It's my favorite. #HisToo

I saved Mommy from a terrifying light that appeared on her phone one night. It was round and bright. But mostly it was new, and that means danger. Video evidence is in the Year Three playlist on my Finn Tube channel! #ImNotSayingItWasAliens #ButItWas

The highlight of the week was getting a gorgeous prezzie in the mail from Mommy's friend, Pat. Pat was one of her very first and very favorite managers at Hewlett Packard, when she was a young'un. She says it's called an intarsia and it's made of cherry, aspen, monkey pod and wenge. Clearly Pat is another artist overwhelmed by my handsomeness and compelled to make my likeness. #WhoCanBlameHim It's hanging on the wall near my other fine art portrait from Julie.
#ImGonnaNeedAGallerySoon #SheWontLetMeLickItThough

That's all the news and #Finnanigans from this week. Over and out.

Week One Hundred Forty-Seven

January 9, 2021 ·

HI EVERYONE. FINN HERE with my week 147 report. It's been a mostly quiet week here at the house of Finn. Mommy made me homemade sweet potato treats and put me in charge of quality control. I performed multiple inspections and deemed them worthy. She was feeling pretty proud of herself about this gourmet dog treat win until Daddy reminded her I used to eat cigarette butts and doll clothing. #HesNotWrong #ImNotVeryDiscriminating

It's been cold and dreary a lot of days, so we've been stuck inside a lot. I made a video about nothing because I was bored. #ItsAboutNothingButImStillAdorable #BigStretch

Daddy and I went for a boys-only walk along the canal early in the week before the dreary weather came. It was really fun, and we went really far. We saw lots of wildlife and bird life on our adventure. It also gave us time to practice not jumping on or screaming at hoomans who pass by without petting me. #ItsSoHard #TheyAreMonsters #BroTimeIsAGoodTime

I also saved the hoomans from the evil broom again! I found it hiding in the closet with my food!!!! I don't know how long it's been hiding in there, but now I'm on high alert every time I walk by. Sometimes I just walk by and growl for good measure. #ImWatchingYouEvilBroom

The highlight of the week was definitely yesterday!! Daddy took me to Heavenly Hound Hotel for a play day!! I saw all my friends and reminded them why I'm called THE KISSY BANDIT. While Kristin gave me a mani/pedi, we talked about what we've each been up to and how we shouldn't go this long in between seeing each other. #WeReallyShouldnt

Then I got to walk over to the other building and see Dr. Richards!! I love her. She gave me the usual once over, checked a freckle on my eye lid #BeacuseMommyIsALevelTenWorrier, and told me I'm delightful. #Duh She and Mommy are still working on my food allergies, so it looks like more homemade meals for me for a while. #ThanksDrR #WarmChickenDontMindIfIDo

I had so much fun at daycare that I refused to leave. Daddy came to get me, and I ran into a crate and refused to go. He called out to me, but I wouldn't make eye contact and refused to even acknowledge I knew this man. #WhatsThatHooman #ICantHearYou #ILiveHereNow
After a few minutes of hooman laughter and begging, the nice lady crawled into the crate to drag me out. #Traitor I hope I get to go back soon. I love playing with my friends there.
#HaveYourHoomansCallMyHoomans

That's all the news and #Finnanigans from this week. Over and out.

Week One Hundred Forty-Eight

January 16, 2021 ·

HI EVERYONE. FINN HERE with my week 148 report. Stella. Stella. Stelllllluuuhhhh. This week's post is dedicated entirely to Stella. Sunday was a good day. I got to visit Stella and her hoomans at their new dwelling. Her Daddy, Richie, is one of my favorite hoomans ever. The view from the deck over the canal is beautiful and there were so many birds to monitor. We even heard an owl! #HootHoot They hadn't moved in yet so there was no furniture to get in our way. We played on the deck, and Stella gave me a tour of the new digs while the hoomans did their own tour. #WhichOneIsMyRoomThough #ThatsRightTheyAllAre

I christened the new dwelling by peeing on their gorgeous stone fireplace inside the house. Mommy FREAKED which made it extra fun. #YoureWelcomeDontMentionIt #NoReallyDontCuzMommyGetsSuperMad

Then on Thursday, while her hoomans handled the move to the new house, Stella came to our house for a playdate. It was our best date yet. We wrastled and played for hours on end. She has so much puppy energy and didn't need breaks as often as me. I designated Mommy as base and would crawl into her lap when I needed a time-out. It was a wonderful day and I think I'm starting to win her back!! Daddy prepared a video montage of our two dates for you!

We got our printed proof copy of the new Field Guide book and Mommy was pleased. She says it's cute and gifty which should help it take off. We also made some progress on my new children's activity/coloring book about dog safety, care and rescues! The illustrator is drawing me into coloring book scenes and showing us as she goes along. It's fun to turn into a cartoon! Dr. K even checked it over to make sure we cover the right points for the littles. #ThanksDrK #LittlesAreMyFavorite

I don't know what's in store for this week, but I hope it's more Stella! #SheCantQuitMe

That's all the news and #Finnanigans from this week. Over and out.

Week One Hundred Forty-Nine

January 23, 2021 ·

HI EVERYONE. FINN HERE with my week 149 report. In super fun news, *Frederick Magazine* did a really nice article about me this month!!! Daddy read it to me and spoiler alert: it's adorable. #JustLikeMe I'm in negotiations with my agent about what level of famousness is required before I get a live-in masseuse. #MyAgentIsAlsoMommy #ShesCrazy #TheNegotiationsAreIntense

Mommy and Daddy left the house for two whole hours on Saturday WITHOUT ME. This hasn't happened in almost a year. It was horrendous, but I found the strength to power through. #JustNotQuietly

Daddy left in the go-for-a-ride very early this morning and I'll admit, I panicked. Mommy seems to think she's some sort of substitute for my Hairy One. #SheIsMistaken

The hoomans have been abuzz with chatter this week. They seem to be making big decisions and dealing with lots of details about something. First, why aren't they consulting me on all major decisions? And second, I don't like the way this distracts them from me. I'm hearing things like

"selling house" and "which furniture to sell" and "how hard it's gonna be to pack up and leave our house." I am not sure what this means, but I'll keep you posted. Mommy says we're going to spend most of February back at the Maryland house doing something she calls "packing and cleaning." I hope we get to see snow again one more time, and I can't wait to pee on everything that needs peeing on there. Most importantly though, Mommy says I get to go play with Scott and the pack at K9 Camp a lot for a few weeks!! I can't wait to give everyone kisses there. I don't know when February is, but I hope it's soon. #ChangeIsHard #KissyBanditSoonReturns

In celebration of the new book releasing this week, I taught Daddy to give me lots of treats when I twirl. Mommy took a slow-motion video that we agree is the cutest thing ever.

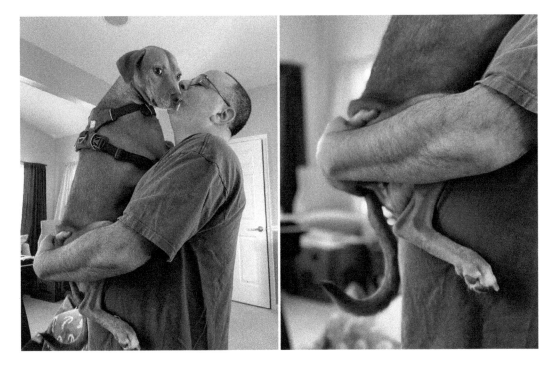

I'm also providing photos snapped by the heinous pawparazzi during some bro-time. You can see the epic shade I threw the photographer for interrupting our sweet moment. #ShesTheWorst

That's all the news and #Finnanigans from this week. Over and out.

Week One Hundred Fifty

January 30, 2021 ·

HI EVERYONE. FINN HERE with my week 150 report. It was a pretty quiet start to the week. We had a little dusting of snow and some frigid arctic temperatures. Daddy and I bundled up like great hunters from the northlands for our parambles. I find running immediately inside and crawling under the covers with Mommy to be the best post-walk warm-up method. Cold paws against warm skin, for the win. #StopItSheLovesIt #EspeciallyWhenShesAsleep

Tuesday evening was a horror show. It was clearly dinner o'clock and no one was moving. I had to get ugly.

Wednesday was really the highlight of the week. Daddy took me to see Stella for a surprise date!! #SheCantQuitMe She showed me all her stuff that's now unpacked in her new house, and we played fetch on the deck. I stole her toys and made her beg me to stop. (Spoiler alert: I didn't.) We had a great time, but the hoomans chaperoned a little too well. #ICouldntMakeMyMove

Things turned very ugly on Thursday. Daddy left in the go-for-a-ride and did not return. We almost died. Stop me if you've heard this one. #NeverMindImGonnaTellYouAgain

That fool drove away and left me alone with the Squishy One. I'm never sure if she can be trusted to feed me, walk me and tend to my needs like the Hairy One. I was not in full melt down until nigh nigh. It was then I realized he wasn't coming back, ever. I tried to comfort Mommy through the night. I could feel her fear and anxiety radiating from within me. #IMustBeAnEmpath I deployed aggressive smothering techniques and periodic ghost/intruder/danger alerts until sunrise. This seemed to help us both. I would lay across her face and she would push me off, putting on a brave face. I would climb onto the top of her head, and she would beg me to "just relax." #HowCanIRelaxWhenWeCouldAllBeDeadByMorning

We rallied at dawn for some brekkie and a freezing cold walk. #BothOfWhichSheDidWrong I was really tired from her shenanigans overnight, so I napped in the sun most of the day. She would occasionally poke me and say things like, "Oh.... are you tired? Gee, me too. How nice that you can nap." #ShesSoAnnoying #YoureWelcomeDevilWoman

Thankfully, Daddy returned home Friday night and all was right in the world again. He asked if I was a good boy for Mommy, and I rolled my eyes. I don't like when he leaves

me in charge of her. And I really don't like how she does anything. #ShesAHotMess

In what I can only assume was an attempt to apologize, the Hairy One took me in the go-for-a-ride to get a pup cup from the donut castle. And it worked. #AllIsForgiven

That's all the news and #Finnanigans from this week. Over and out.

Week One Hundred Fifty-One

February 6, 2021 ·

HI EVERYONE. FINN HERE with my week 151 report. I got to thinking that I hadn't seen Dr. Richards and my friends at Coastal Vet in a while. So I thought long and hard until I grew a bump on top of my thinker. This made Mommy worry and get me a rush appointment. #Bonus Dr. Richards gave me my customary belly rub and told me I'm the handsomest. She thinks the bump is an accidental love bite from a certain lady friend that just needs to heal. #LoveHurts #WorthIt #Stellluhhh I stopped by the salon on the way out and got a quick pawticure. The ladies told me I'm a good boy while they cleaned me up. Gotta stay looking good in case of another surprise Stella date! A good time was had by all. #LLFinn

The snow finally found us at the formerly-alternate, now primary, dwelling. More on that in a minute. We had a great time playing in the snow, and I ate as much as I could until the brain-freeze kicked in. Mmmm. Snow-covered grass is my favorite grass. My second favorite grass is lawnmower cakes. I digress. I love it when Daddy barks, "It's not a buffet, Finn!!!!" #GrassDistractsMe #SnacksAreLife

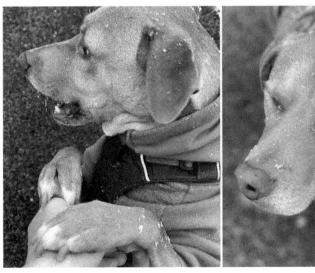

The last week has been full of things I don't like. I like things where they belong and just so.
#ThisIsJustSoWrong

Mommy said that we're selling our primary dwelling. She and Daddy have been moving furniture, packing things, and putting things where they don't go. They even took the door off the hinges in our bedroom to get something big out. I don't like it. They are also refusing to let me run things.
#ImTheBossThoughSoIDoAnyway

Strange people are coming to the house to take things, and I'm not even allowed to kiss them! How can I possibly evaluate their suspiciousness or deliciousness

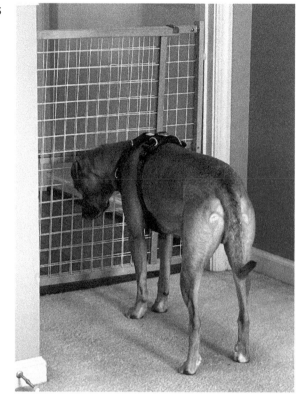

from another room behind this gate thing? #TheyreDoingThisAllWrong
#WhyArentTheyRequiringTreatsInSalePrices

Mommy says this madness will be going on for a few weeks, and I need to be brave and halpful. I plan to contribute my usual demand for constant attention, step on her while she's packing boxes, and be generally loud and distracting. I will miss the primary dwelling. #IThinkTheyWillToo

In other news, I've recently decided that my least favorite word, after baff, is stay. There's been a whole lotta, "Finn, stay!" "I mean it, Finn." "Finnnnn sttttaaaaaay." YOU stay, Devil Woman. #IDoWhatIWant I plan to devote some training time this week into this issue. #TheyRequireConstantUpkeep

That's all the news and #Finnanigans from this week. Over and out.

Week One Hundred Fifty-Two

February 13, 2021 ·

HI EVERYONE. FINN HERE with my week 152 report. 250 of my new book, "How to Train Your Hooman" came! Mommy and I pawtographed a whole lotta books this week and started shipping to everyone! Daddy made deliveries to all the awesome local stores that carry them, too. It's really fun to see a new book for the first time!! I also liked that most of my inscriptions were to dogs this time. #NoOffenseHoomans #WhatsYourFavoritePart

We also got the new "Fun with Finn Activity Book: All About Dogs" out to advanced readers this week. And the reviews so far have been pawsome. I can't wait for that to get out into the world and teach the littles how to be dog super heroes. You can order it on Amazon starting today!!!! Just in time for Easter. The illustrator made such beautiful drawings of me and my frens! #MoreMeForEveryone #TheLittlesNeedMe

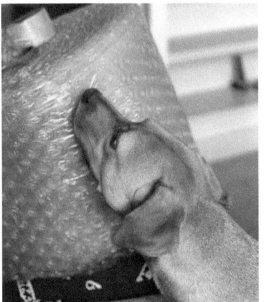

Move-maggedon continues, and we are very busy now packing boxes and sorting things. This is very stressful, but the upside is Mommy has way less time and energy to be pawparrazzi! The downside is she is missing a lot of adorable moments over here. #TheyreAllAdorable

I'm in charge of inspecting every single box as they make it and also after it's taped shut. I pay special attention to the little punch-outs on the sides where the hooman paws carry it. Those interest me in every single box. I'm also in charge of sniffing each item as it goes in, and sometimes, I take stuff back out. #QualityControl #NeedsACloserLook

As usual, Captain Micromanager over here is all over me about "backwards progress," and "the objective is in the box, Finn, not out." Wah wah wah, Devil Woman. We all have our roles here, and mine is the only one that matters. It's so frustrating when she takes something I JUST took out of a box and puts it back in. #ShesAMonster

I've been paying careful attention to Daddy and his stress levels. We've been playing a lot in a big space in our room where a sofa used to be. It's now our own personal WWF ring, and I'm here for it. We play every night and keep Mommy awake. #ShesAWhiner #DaddyNeedsPlayTime

I don't know how long box-mania will be going on but it seems like a long while. Mommy is starting on piles of doguments and files from her office today. #ShesAlsoAHoarder #IHalpWithShredding

Mommy and I are also excited to be doing a virtual author chat in partnership with the iconic Browseabout Bookstore and the Lewes Public Library. Browseabout sent me this pic of their event table showing how famous I am now. Look at all these important and significant books, honored to be alongside me in a Viking hat talking about training your hooman. #IGiveThemCredibility

I hope everypawdy has a good week. I'll just be over here trying to keep these hoomans in line. #DontCallMeAHero #OkDoActually

That's all the news and #Finnanigans from this week. Over and out.

Week One Hundred Fifty-Three

February 20, 2021 ·

HI EVERYONE. FINN HERE with my week 153 report.
#Movemaggedon2021 is really getting to me. I'm having fits and crying
even when Mommy is holding me. That makes her sad, which makes me sad.
#WeAreAMess It's really stressful with all the chaos and my stuff going in
boxes. I regret to report that I've been stress-eating my frens at an alarming
rate to cope with the anxiety of this moving stuff. I'm also anxiety-licking
Mommy, and she's starting to crack about it. #ICantHalpIt #ItsSoothing
#HoldStill

Uncle Al came by and gave me lovin's. I haven't seen him in many nigh nighs.
I couldn't get to his face for kisses because of his COVID mask. This frustrated
me, but I liked trying anyway. #YOUGetDownDevilWoman

Best of all I got to go to K9 camp this week!! I saw all my frens and made some new ones. Everyone was happy to see me and I played 'til I dropped! #TheKissyBanditReturns

Friday was my 4th barkday. THERE WAS NO CAKE. No frozen dairy slop, no cake, nothing homemade. Mommy says she'll make it up to me after #movemaggeddon2021 is over, but I'm not buying it. All I got was this lousy hot dog. #StickingACandleInItDoesntMakeItCake #ShesDeadToMe #CakesAreTheONEThingShesGoodFor

But I was gracious anyway. See evidence here: https://youtu.be/KUoEewnClo8 The white fluffy stuff came down like crazy this week and that was super fun. Daddy and I played in my fenced area, and I loved it. We barked at stuff, chased geese and ruled the yard! #ImASnowEater

That's all the news and #Finnanigans from this week. Over and out.

Week One Hundred Fifty-Four

February 27, 2021 ·

YOU DON'T NEED TO REPEAT YOURSELF.

I IGNORED YOU JUST FINE THE FIRST TIME.

@FINNCHRONICLES

HI EVERYONE. FINN HERE with my week 154 report. I got to go to a fascinating concrete jungle of captive hoomans called Lowe's. It was a huge warehouse of hoomans and dangerous stuff. I know this because every time I tried to scale a shelf or lick something, Daddy said, "No Finn, that's dangerous." #HesSoBrave There were so many hoomans there to pet me!! Daddy and I went to the paint counter so they could fawn over me to get things started. Then we walked up and down the aisles of danger to show our bravery and collect hooman adoration. #LickedStuff #LikedIt #KnockedOneThingOver #ItWasExhilarating

If any hooman passed by, I screamed and howled to remind them I was there, ready to be adored. #TheAcousticsWereAmazing Several hoomans decorated with blue vests brought me treats and told me I was the cutest. I gather that the blue vests indicate some act of bravery or maybe an escalated position of power in the concrete jungle social construct. One would come find me then tell others, and soon I had a swoon of blue vesters attending to me appropriately. #AreYouMyNewStaff #YesILikeEarScratchesYouFool #RightThereIsGood

I also got lots of garage visitors this week. I haven't seen too many hoomans since the pandemic started, but this week was hooman-palooza!! Michelle and Michael came to see me and we let loose with wiggles and kisses in the

garage. Michelle has the best laugh and lets me lick her face off. Laura and John also came to see me and got some garage love. They halped Mommy move heavy things and tried to remind me about not jumping on hoomans. #ItDidntWork #GoodTryThough I also met a nice lady named Tara who has triplet littles and one bigger little. She smelled like heaven. I finally got to meet Raimi and Ryan, too! Raimi takes care of dogs and smelled like a glorious plume of dog hair and treats. Andrea also came over, and I mauled her trying to get her mask off. Wayne and MaryAnn came for a visit, too!! The only problem was that everyone had on masks that blocked my access to my favorite part of the hoomans!?!? #GimmeYourPieHole #AggressiveKisserNeedsFullFaceAccess

I saved my hoomans from not one but TWO broom monsters in the hallway. They must have followed us here from the other house. #IHateBrooms #ISaveYou

I think #Movemaggedon2021 is almost over. The stress of it has really gotten to me. I had lots of goodbye kissies and tears from hoomans this week. Everyone at camp gave me kissies and told me they would miss me. I gave Scott extra kissies and tried to tell him how much I love him. Then I went to see Dr K and she did the same thing. I could feel everyone's sadness and it made me sad, too. Mommy assures me that we will go back for visits and to see our friends again. I hope we do. #FrederickFriendsAreForever

My favorite part of the week, though, has been seeing all the pictures of the

littles coloring in my new activity book!!! Each time someone sends Mommy a picture of their little with a drawing, a colored page, or solving a puzzle, we both get very excited. We still can't believe we made that! A Humane Society in New York wants to use the books for a fundraiser this summer focused on teaching littles about dog care and safety. Yay!!! Keep posting your pics and tell us what you think of the activity book! It makes us so happy to see!! #EndorphineRushEachTime #FinnFansAreFabulous

That's all the news and #Finnanigans from this week. Over and out.

Week One Hundred Fifty-Five

March 6, 2021 ·

HI EVERYONE. FINN HERE with my week 155 report. The cardboard boxes somehow figured out where we live now and followed us here. There's some kind of sorcery apaw. Some of our furniture also followed us here, and it's confusing for me. Mommy says the madness is over now, and I just have to get used to our new normal. #ShesDelusional #DemonBoxesArentNormal

I rode out the storm in my fortress of solitude while strange men carried the demon boxes into the house. The hoomans seemed to be encouraging their random and unpredictable movements, and I just couldn't take it anymore. I decided if they didn't care enough to have proper management and oversight, I shouldn't either. I did give off an occasional growl to let them know I was watching them. #ImNotALunatic #IWasFedUp #SelfCareIsHealthy

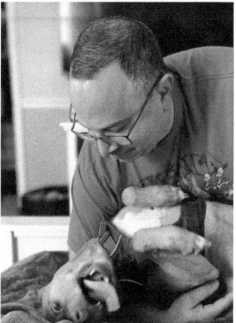

The hoomans spent most of the week unpacking the demon boxes and making more mess. I spent most of the week introducing my formerly primary dwelling frens to my formerly alternate, now primary dwelling frens. Fleet Admiral Fiona and Abominable Snowman did not hit it off, and there's been tension all week. #ILoveTheDrama #HesDownToOneArm #WhoWillWin

The highlight of the week was definitely yesterday. Mommy had some medical thing to do all day, so I got to go to daycare and see my frens! I played with Hulk and Taco for hours. I was so exhausted, but when Jess announced that we were going to have a special date night and for a ride in her Jeep, I lost my mind. Just me and Jess for some quality time? A ride in her Jeep full of kitty glitter? What a treat! I love getting in the backseat and sniffing in all the kitty smells. #ILoveKitties #AndRides #AndJess

I'm embarrassed to say that I wasn't a very good date once we got back to my place. Jess made us a lovely dinner. I was so tired I just ate then crashed. She stayed here watching me sleep until the pawrents got home. #Creepy #ShesObsessedWithMe #LLFinn #BipedGirlfriend #StellaIsMyFurGirlfriendStillThough

I'm sorry there aren't more pics and videos this week. Mommy has been very distracted. She danced around to a FloRida song this morning while cleaning the kitchen and kept trying to take my picture. But I didn't want to cooperate. I refuse to reward her behavior. #PawparazziTryinToMakeMePose #PutYourPawsUp

That's all the news and #Finnanigans from this week. Over and out.

Week One Hundred Fifty-Six

March 13, 2021 ·

HI EVERYONE. FINN HERE with my week 156 report. It's hard to believe, but it's been three years this week since I rescued these hoomans. Wednesday was their third gotchaversary. We celebrated on Sunday with a pupcake from Sandy Pawz in Bethany Beach and a romp on the sand. I picked out a new argyle collar and matching leash to mark the occasion and we strolled the boards demanding affection.
#ItWorksEveryTime #WhyYesYouMayPetMe

We had a nice week-long acknowledgment of our three years together. Most importantly, things from the move have mostly settled down, and I'm back to being the center of attention.
#AsItShouldBe

We hit the local bookstores from Bethany up to Rehoboth Thursday evening to deliver my new activity book for the littles. Devil Woman insisted on photo after photo because she was so excited to be out of the house. You can see I refused to give her a single smile. #Disgusted
#NoIDontWanna #PawparazziIsTheWorst

We met some nice people in front of Browseabout Books in Rehoboth. After a nice lady tried to pet me but I was too excited not to jump, she asked how many months old I am. The pawrents laughed and said 48. She looked confused then laughed, too. This happens a lot. #UnsureWhy We caught a beautiful sunset on the way home and Devil Woman tried again for pics. I again refused. #LookWhereYouSay
#IKnowYoureLyingAboutTheCheese

I also finally mastered my remote control game. It took a lot of practice, but I'm finally able to lay on (conceal) the TV remote without pushing any

buttons (alerting the hoomans I'm hiding it). It's thrilling to watch them search about for it and carry on. The only hiccup has been some sorcery that makes it beep and boop underneath me. Mommy said I was super cute while I figured things out and took decisive action to save us.
#ISavedUsThough #DemonRemote

That's all the news and #Finnanigans from this week and year three!

If you laughed, please please please leave a review online where books are sold. Reviews are HUGELY important to indie authors! Over and out.

Acknowledgements

Finn wants to thank a few key people and organizations:

A huge thanks to the Vizsla- and Beagle-loving communities on Facebook, friends and other authors that have followed Finn's updates from the beginning, encouraged us, given us advice during training struggles, sent us surprise packages, and kept nudging me to publish.

Most importantly… the rescues! Vizslas, in particular, are sensitive and intense dogs that need special owners and special support when in rescue. Their emotional nature makes the inconsistency and fear of unstable situations especially traumatic. Finn hopes you'll consider volunteering for or donating to the rescues listed below to help save dogs just like him. If every reader donates just $5, imagine how many dogs can be helped! We personally know, love, and trust the dedicated heroes at:

Airsong's Angels, Inc. is an all-volunteer, 501(c)3 non-profit organization and Georgia State Licensed Animal Rescue dedicated to improving the lives of the vizslas in their care by bringing them current on vaccinations, attending to their medical and behavioral needs, providing for spay/neuter, and carefully rehoming them into loving, furever families. https://airsongsangelsinc.org/

Cane Rosso Rescue is a Dallas, TX, based 501(c)3 non-profit organization dedicated to raising funds and building awareness for dogs in need of homes in Texas. The goal of Cane Rosso Rescue is to find homes for dogs that have been abandoned at shelters or whose owners can no longer care for them. We are looking for fosters, adopters, and volunteers to help transport dogs to their future homes. Donations are accepted via Paypal to rescue@canerosso.com to assist with medical care and other expenses. https://www.canerossorescue.org/

Colorado/Wyoming Vizsla Rescue Group, Inc. is a 501(c)3 non-profit organization and Colorado State Licensed Animal Rescue officially formed in 2007. Their mission is to protect the Vizsla who has been abandoned or abused and assist animal rescue organizations that handle Vizslas in need of care due to natural disasters or other emergencies. Their coverage area includes Colorado, Wyoming, western Kansas, western Nebraska, and

New Mexico – but generously assist and support other states when the need arises. https://www.coloradovizsla.org/

Conestoga Vizsla Club (CVC) New Beginnings is a Virginia-based non-profit rescue group that helps Vizslas in need, primarily in the Virginia, Maryland, Delaware, and DC region. https://cvcweb.org/Rescue

About the Author

Finn's dutiful transcriber, Gwen Romack (aka The Squishy One), is a Maryland native, avid dog lover, and rescue volunteer.

Gwen and her husband Evan (aka The Hairy One) agreed to foster Finn a year after losing their beloved Vizsla/Pit mix, Mr. Snuggles, at age 14. She began posting Finn's weekly updates on Facebook as a way to help prospective adopters fall in love with Finn. However, it was clear pretty quickly that she and her husband would become foster fails. Finn was already home! The posts became so popular in the Vizsla community that she decided to continue his weekly updates on the frustrations of a dog rescuing his difficult hoomans.

In 2020, the books were turned into "The Finn Chronicles" series that each catalogue a year in Finn's life and adventures. As Finn's popularity grew and the books took off, Finn's fans started asking for more. Finn now guest-teaches to littles all over the country via Zoom and has started writing new books like this one. Finn and Gwen love hearing the stories from fans of all ages about how much joy he brings them.

At the time of publishing, sweet and sassy Finn is in year four of weekly updates. If the books do well, Gwen plans to keep publishing subsequent years and donate a portion of the proceeds to Finn's favorite rescue organizations.

KEEP THE FUN GOING

To learn more about me and my other hilarious books, check out my media coverage, how we donate time to schools, and how to follow me for daily fun on social media, scan this barcode with your phone or go to www.linktr.ee/gwenromack and have fun exploring!

And don't forget to sign up to be a FINNatic on my website to get the latest news on everything FINN!

Do you know a little hooman who could use a brain workout? Check out my *FUN WITH FINN ACTIVITY BOOK: ALL ABOUT DOGS* that teaches kids all about dogs! A wonderful illustrator named Jean

Tower drew me throughout and as usual, I look stunning! The book includes real frens from my life that you'll recognize, a maze, a crossword, a cipher code, math squares, a search word, a hidden objects picture, coloring pages, matching columns, find what's different between two drawings, a gratitude page, and more. We cover unsafe foods for dogs, good and bad behavior when interacting with dogs, how rescue organizations help special dogs and how much we love our veterinarians! A special veterinarian, teacher, rescue organization and mom consulted to make sure the book covers all the right things! And, it's fun!

These are my other fun books for full-sized hoomans!

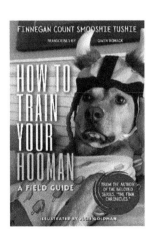

NOW GO FIND A DOG AND GIVE THEM A TREAT! #STAT

If this book made you smile, please consider leaving a review online. Reviews and ratings are critical to indie authors!!!! Thank you!

CPSIA information can be obtained
at www.ICGtesting.com
Printed in the USA
LVHW070034251121
704425LV00005B/88